ESPECIALLY FOR:

_____

FROM:

_____

DATE:

_____

3-Minute Devotions for COURAGEOUS Girls

JOANNE SIMMONS

BARBOUR **kidz**
A Division of Barbour Publishing

© 2021 by Barbour Publishing, Inc.

ISBN 978-1-64352-707-9

Published by Barbour Publishing, Inc., 1810 Barbour Drive, Uhrichsville, Ohio 44683, www.barbourbooks.com

Our mission is to inspire the world with the life-changing message of the Bible.

Member of the
Evangelical Christian
Publishers Association

Printed in the United States of America.

000575 1220 SP

3 MINUTES TO A COURAGEOUS HEART

These devotions were written especially for courageous girls like you. Just three tiny minutes are all you need to make a connection with God, the Courage Giver!

- Minute 1: Read the day's Bible verse and reflect on what God's Word is saying.
- Minute 2: Read the devotion and think about what it means for your life.
- Minute 3: Pray. . .and grow closer to God!

Turn the page and discover how 180 seconds of quiet time with God can change your life!

GOD WON'T FAIL YOU

*"Be strong and courageous, and do the work.
Don't be afraid or discouraged, for the Lord God,
my God, is with you. He will not fail you."*
1 Chronicles 28:20 NLT

♡♡

I need courage to write this book for you to read. Every time I begin to write, I'm a little scared as I think, *How do I fill up these blank pages with words that matter and bring glory to God?*

All kinds of situations require great courage— some that might seem silly and small and others that are huge. Whatever is going on in your life, God won't fail you. I pray this book helps you see what a courageous girl you are when you let God live in you, love you, and empower you!

. . . .

*Dear God, You are the creator and giver of all courage.
Help me to be a courageous girl because of You living
in me, loving me, and empowering me. Amen.*

BELIEVE AND BE SAVED, PART 1

"Believe in the Lord Jesus and you will be saved."
ACTS 16:31 NLT

So, how exactly does the creator of all courage live in and love you and empower you? First by being sure you have accepted Jesus Christ as your Savior.

- Do you believe that there is only one true God?
- Do you believe that Jesus is God and came to earth as a baby to live a perfect life?
- Do you admit that you make mistakes and are a sinner?
- Do you believe Jesus died on the cross to forgive you of your sin?
- Do you believe Jesus rose to life again and offers eternal life to all who believe in Him as the one and only Savior from sin?
- Do you believe you should give your life to Jesus and live it for Him, following His ways?

Even if you are not sure yet, you can keep on thinking and praying about these things. Read God's Word more and more and ask questions of people you know who love Jesus.

....

Dear God, I want to believe all of these things!
Please help me. Please grow my faith in You. Amen.

BELIEVE AND BE SAVED,
PART 2

*God so loved the world that he gave his one
and only Son, that whoever believes in him
shall not perish but have eternal life.*
JOHN 3:16 NIV

If your answer to *all* of those questions in the previous devotional is truly yes and you have prayed to God about your answers to the questions and asked Jesus into your life, then

- you are saved from your sin;
- you have the promise of life forever in heaven; and
- in this world you have the help and power and courage of God's Holy Spirit with you every second of every day.

How incredibly awesome is that?

*Dear Jesus, I believe that You are God and that You
lived a sinless human life on earth. Then You died on
the cross to cover all of my sin. Then You rose again,
and You give me eternal life and constant help and
power through Your Holy Spirit. I believe in You,
Jesus, as my one and only Savior! Thank You! Amen.*

BRAVERY FOR BAPTISM, PART 1

Jesus came to them and said: I have been given all authority in heaven and on earth! Go to the people of all nations and make them my disciples. Baptize them in the name of the Father, the Son, and the Holy Spirit.
MATTHEW 28:18–19 CEV

♡♡

If you have accepted Jesus as your Savior, a brave next step is to be baptized. Baptism is a symbol with water that represents getting rid of sin and having new life in Jesus! It's like the very best kind of bath! It's not something you have to do to be saved from your sins. Think of the man on the cross beside Jesus, for example. He never had a chance to be baptized with water, and Jesus told him he would be with Him that very day in heaven! (Luke 23:42–43). But baptism is a beautiful and brave thing to do if you have asked Jesus to be your Savior.

....

Dear God, Your Word talks about baptism, and I want to learn more about it. Please help me to understand the significance of baptism. Amen.

BRAVERY FOR BAPTISM, PART 2

Jesus answered, "For now this is how it should be, because we must do all that God wants us to do." Then John agreed. So Jesus was baptized. And as soon as he came out of the water, the sky opened, and he saw the Spirit of God coming down on him like a dove. Then a voice from heaven said, "This is my own dear Son, and I am pleased with him."
MATTHEW 3:15–17 CEV

If you are able and have the chance, baptism shows that you want to obey God and be like Jesus. It shows that you are saved from sin and are a follower of Jesus! Christians who bravely get baptized help inspire others to trust in Jesus as Savior too. If you are interested in baptism, talk to your parents and your leaders at church.

Dear Jesus, the Bible says You were baptized and You encouraged others to be baptized. Give me courage to be like You and to obey God in all things! Amen.

HOLY SPIRIT POWER

*May the power of the Holy
Spirit fill you with hope.*
ROMANS 15:13 CEV

When you believe in Jesus and accept Him as Savior, you are given an amazing gift, better than your favorite birthday or Christmas gift! It's the gift of God's Holy Spirit to live in you and guide you! Ephesians 1:13–14 (NLV) says, "The truth is the Good News. When you heard the truth, you put your trust in Christ. Then God marked you by giving you His Holy Spirit as a promise. The Holy Spirit was given to us as a promise that we will receive everything God has for us."

If you are ever feeling scared or worried about anything, but you know you have accepted Jesus as your Savior, then do this: Stop for a moment. Close your eyes. Take a deep breath. Then focus on the fact that the all-powerful, all-knowing creator God is living in you! Remind yourself of that regularly so that you will have constant courage and hope, no matter what situation you are facing.

Dear God, You are living in me through Your Holy Spirit. I don't ever want to forget that. Strengthen me again and again with Your great power, courage, and hope! Amen.

LIKE SUPERHEROES

For God did not give us a spirit of fear. He gave
us a spirit of power and of love and of a good mind.
2 TIMOTHY 1:7 NLV

♡♡

If you were given a superpower, like in a superhero movie, what power would you want? And if you got it, would you want to sit around and never use it? Of course not! You'd fly if you could, right? And what would you do if you could be invisible? And *when* would you go if you could time travel?

Now think about how God has given you His superpower of the Holy Spirit in you. You don't just want to sit around doing nothing with that, do you? Ask God every day what brave and powerful things He wants to do through you! How does He want you to share and serve and help people to spread His encouragement and love?

. . . .

Dear God, in a way, You truly have made me a superhero
because You are in me through Your Holy Spirit. I want
to live for You and serve You with all the good gifts and
talents You have given me. Show me each day the things
You want me to do, all to give You praise! Amen.

LET THE BIBLE MAKE YOU BRAVE

All Scripture is inspired by God and is useful to teach us what is true and to make us realize what is wrong in our lives. It corrects us when we are wrong and teaches us to do what is right. God uses it to prepare and equip his people to do every good work.
2 TIMOTHY 3:16–17 NLT

God loves to encourage us in many ways, and especially with words, for He gave us His Word, the Bible, which is the best and most popular book in history. The Bible is God's main way of speaking to people. It's not just some ancient book that doesn't matter for today. It has been changing lives for thousands of years. Hebrews 4:12 (NLT) says, "The word of God is alive and powerful." No other book is living! So spend time reading God's Word and letting it speak to you. With the combination of the Holy Spirit living and working in you and God's Word in your mind and heart, you are equipped with power and courage to face anything that comes your way!

Dear God, thank You for speaking to me through Your Word. Help me to love it, read it, and memorize it. Let the Bible make me brave. Amen.

TRUSTING GOD'S WORD

*We always thank God that when you heard the Word
of God from us, you believed it. You did not receive it as
from men, but you received it as the Word of God. That
is what it is. It is at work in the lives of you who believe.*
1 THESSALONIANS 2:13 NLV

♡♡

You might wonder sometimes, *How do I know the Bible
is true? Why should I trust it to help give me courage?* If
you take time to look, you will find amazing research
from experts throughout history who verify why the
Bible can be trusted far more than any other book
ever written. Check out great resources like Answers
in Genesis and author Josh McDowell for more good
info. More importantly, constantly remember that
you have a relationship with God Himself through
Jesus Christ and you have the Holy Spirit in you. As
you read the Bible consistently over time, ask God to
show more and more of Himself to you through His
Word. Ask Him to grow your faith, and then trust Him
to do it, and you will be amazed at how He answers
your prayers.

*Dear God, please keep growing my faith
in You as I read Your awesome Word!
Show me how and why it's true. Amen.*

COURAGE WHEN THE PLANS
SEEM CRAZY, PART 1

*The LORD was pleased with Noah, and this
is the story about him. Noah was the only
person who lived right and obeyed God.*
GENESIS 6:8–9 CEV

You've probably heard about Noah and how he was the one good guy in a world full of bad guys. The Bible says God was pleased with Noah, and then God gave Noah some instructions that must have seemed totally crazy! Build a giant ark? Collect two of each animal and load them up along with the family? Then wait while the rains fall and totally flood and destroy the earth? Even though Noah was such a good man, I bet he shook his head sometimes, wondering what on earth was going on!

*Dear God, even when I'm confused and feel
like the plans seem crazy, give me the courage
to keep trusting and obeying You! Amen.*

COURAGE WHEN THE PLANS SEEM CRAZY, PART 2

Noah did everything the LORD told him to do.
GENESIS 6:22 CEV

♡♡

Even if the plans seemed crazy to Noah, he continued to obey God, and that took a whole lot of courage. In the end, God did exactly what He said He would do: He destroyed every living thing with a great flood. Only Noah and his family and the animals they had gathered survived, safe inside the ark. Noah could look back and be thankful he was brave enough to continue to obey God when he sure didn't understand.

At times God will direct you to do things that might seem to make *zero* sense, but they are part of God's plan. So keep on being brave and obeying your good heavenly Father!

. . . .

Dear God, remind me that I don't need to know all of Your plans to trust and obey You. I know that everything You do is good and right. I love You and want to follow You in anything that You ask of me. Amen.

COOLEST KIND OF LIFE

*God planned for us to do good things and
to live as he has always wanted us to live.*
EPHESIANS 2:10 CEV

Choosing to trust in Jesus and live for Him requires a lot of courage. To really follow Him and His Word means to do a lot of things differently than what our world and popular culture says is good and cool. You might get made fun of. You might lose friends. You might be totally misunderstood. You might be left out or rejected or passed up for opportunities. In spite of all that, there is nothing better than knowing and living for the One who created you and has great plans for you! His ways are higher and better than the best thing this world has to offer, and He will put you in the places He wants you to be. Keep asking Him to show you His plans and His purpose for you, and then do them—because that is the very coolest, most courageous kind of life.

....

*Dear God, I want what You want for me more than
anything else. Give me new courage each day to keep
choosing You and Your ways over the ways of this world.
I want to follow You and live for You alone! Amen.*

DON'T PUT IT OFF

*Give all your cares to the Lord
and He will give you strength.*
PSALM 55:22 NLV

Have you ever tried to avoid what makes you anxious or scared? I sure have! In college I knew I had to take a public speaking class, one that most people took in their freshman year. But since it made me so nervous, I kept putting it off until my senior year. Guess what? I was still nervous about it once I finally took the class, and maybe even a little embarrassed too. Avoiding it for three years did nothing to help the situation. I should have just confronted the fear, asked God for extra courage, and got the class finished in my first year, and then I wouldn't have had the worry of it hanging around in my head for three years!

When you find yourself regularly worried or scared about something, ask God to help you confront the fear rather than avoid it. Facing it will let you see how God's power can work through you to overcome! He loves you and wants to help you with everything!

....

*Dear God, with You working in me, I want
to face fear and worry, not try to avoid it.
Please give me courage and help me! Amen.*

THE COURAGE OF THE MIDWIVES, PART 1

Because the midwives feared God, they refused to obey the king's orders. They allowed the boys to live.
EXODUS 1:17 NLT

Shiphrah and Puah—those are interesting names, right? They are the names of two incredibly courageous women in the Bible. During the time when God's people, the Israelites, lived in Egypt, a king, also known as a pharaoh, decided there were too many of them. He was afraid the Israelites would join together to take away his power. So he made all the Israelites slaves, and he made sure they were treated cruelly. The pharaoh even ordered that every new baby boy born to an Israelite mother must be killed. But two of the midwives, the women who helped new moms as they delivered their babies, named Shiphrah and Puah, respected God and secretly refused to kill babies.

Dear God, thank You for the example of Shiphrah and Puah, who showed great courage to defy an evil king to save the lives of many of Your people. Amen.

THE COURAGE OF THE MIDWIVES, PART 2

The king of Egypt called for the midwives. "Why have you done this?" he demanded. "Why have you allowed the boys to live?" "The Hebrew women are not like the Egyptian women," the midwives replied. "They are more vigorous and have their babies so quickly that we cannot get there in time." So God was good to the midwives, and the Israelites continued to multiply, growing more and more powerful. And because the midwives feared God, he gave them families of their own.
EXODUS 1:18–21 NLT

Shiphrah and Puah had to appear before the king of Egypt and explain why they had allowed the baby boys to live. And they made up a lie to defy Pharaoh and keep protecting the baby boys. Usually it's never good to lie, but in this case God blessed the midwives for their great courage to do so because the lie protected the innocent, helpless baby boys of His people. And through this courage of two women, the man who would lead the Israelites out of Egypt—Moses—was safely born to his mother, Jochebed.

Dear God, please give me wisdom and courage, and work through me in brave ways like You did Shiphrah and Puah. Amen.

BLESSINGS ON TOP

*God will give you everything you need
because of His great riches in Christ Jesus.*
PHILIPPIANS 4:19 NLV

Do you love to get frozen yogurt and pile on amazing toppings? My favorite are the boba! Froyo is yummy on its own but definitely even better with lots of little treats on top!

I love how God gives us good blessings and then often piles extras on top. When you're needing extra courage in a hard situation, sometimes you need to take time to focus on the blessings you have and then the extra-special blessings God has piled on top. Write them down and pray over them with thankfulness. Gratitude for what God has done and what He has given you in the past is a great way to build hope and courage for how He is going to supply again for your needs right now and in the future!

....

*Dear God, thank You for my many blessings. Thank You
for all the ways You've given to me and helped me in
the past that help me believe for all the ways You will
keep on giving and blessing in the future. Amen.*

CONFRONT AND COMMUNICATE

"If your brother sins against you, go and tell him what he did without other people hearing it. If he listens to you, you have won your brother back again. But if he will not listen to you, take one or two other people with you."
MATTHEW 18:15–16 NLV

Have you ever been afraid to face a person who keeps causing you worry or fear? Ask God to give you wisdom about how to confront them. You might need to get a parent or other trusted grown-up involved too. Ask God to show you exactly the right people to help. And ask Him for good communication when you do confront the person. So many times, worry and fear are based on bad communication, but talking things out in good ways is a wonderful way to fix problems!

Sometimes confronting and communicating do not work out the way you might hope. But you can have peace knowing that you tried, and you can let God strengthen and grow you through the process.

Dear God, I need courage to confront other people sometimes. Please show me how to do it in wise and helpful ways. Help me to communicate well. Amen.

GO-TO GROUP

*If you have sinned, you should tell each
other what you have done. Then you can
pray for one another and be healed.*
JAMES 5:16 CEV

Do you have a go-to group of people whom you can
talk to about anything? Family and friends you can
trust? I hope so! If you are facing a stressful or scary
situation, don't keep it a secret from them. Talking
about fears and worries usually helps a problem or
concern seem far less scary. And make sure you're
asking your go-to group to pray with you and for you.
Each prayer from your loved ones is a boost to your
confidence and courage, coming from God as He
hears each prayer and reaches out to help.

*Dear God, thank You for family and friends who love me,
support me, and pray for me. Please always give me
this kind of people in my life. Thank You for the way
You give me help and courage through them. Amen.*

A MOTHER'S COURAGE, PART 1

*She put the baby in the basket and laid it among
the reeds along the bank of the Nile River.*
EXODUS 2:3 NLT

♡♡

Jochebed loved and cared for her baby boy (who would later be named Moses) and kept him safe for three months. But as he grew, he became too big to hide. So Jochebed placed her son inside a waterproof basket and put it among the reeds near the edge of the Nile River. She knew that Pharaoh's daughter often came there. Jochebed asked her daughter, Miriam, to watch and see what happened. Soon the princess spotted the basket and found the baby crying and felt sorry for him.

Miriam asked the princess, "Do you want me to find a mother who can feed him for you?"

And the princess agreed. So Miriam brought Jochebed to the princess.

The princess said, "I will pay you to take care of him for me until he can eat on his own." She had no idea she was talking to the baby's real mother! But God knew.

....

*Dear God, this story helps show me how much You
care about Your people—and I know that means
You care so much about me too! Thank You! Amen.*

A MOTHER'S COURAGE, PART 2

*So the woman took her baby home and nursed him.
Later, when the boy was older, his mother brought
him back to Pharaoh's daughter, who adopted him
as her own son. The princess named him Moses,
for she explained, "I lifted him out of the water."*
EXODUS 2:9–10 NLT

♡♡

Jochebed happily agreed to the princess's plan, and she got to spend more time with her son. Then when baby Moses grew old enough, Jochebed gave him back to Pharaoh's daughter.

Jochebed's heart must have hurt to give up her son, but more important than her own heart was protecting her child and obeying God's plans. Because of his mother's courage, Moses' life was saved from Pharaoh's evil plans, and Moses grew to be one of God's greatest leaders of all time.

....

*Dear God, thank You for the example
of Jochebed, who showed great courage
by protecting her son. Amen.*

WORD IN A WORD

Encourage one another and build one another up.
1 THESSALONIANS 5:11 ESV

Think of a time when you really needed some extra encouragement and then you got it. What happened? Did you get a card in the mail from a friend "just because"? Maybe Mom and Dad took you out for ice cream as a fun surprise. Maybe a teacher noticed how hard you worked on a project and celebrated with you in class. Whatever it was, think of how it made you feel. Encouragement fills you with happiness and confidence. Also, did you notice that the word *courage* is in the word *encouragement*? Yes, when someone encourages you, it helps you feel brave too—brave to face anything because you know you have people who love and care about you and will always support and cheer you on.

So next time you encourage someone in even the simplest way, and when you receive any kind of encouragement, think about how it's not just to spread something cheerful but to help others be brave to face any hard thing.

Dear God, thank You for the encouragers in my life, and help me to be an encourager too. Amen.

COURAGEOUSLY COMMITTED

Should we keep on sinning, so that God's wonderful kindness will show up even better? No, we should not!
ROMANS 6:1–2 CEV

Some people wonder why it matters what kind of choices they make since Jesus has saved people from sin. They might think it's no big deal to make bad choices and disobey God's Word. They just want to do what everyone else in the world says is popular and fun. But no matter how much love and forgiveness God gives, bad choices always have consequences. So anyone who says they are a Christian but does not do their best to obey God's ways will certainly have a lot of trouble in their lives.

However, doing your best to obey God's Word does not mean a perfect life with zero trouble. But it does mean God helps you through every trouble and works everything out for good for those who love Him (Romans 8:28).

Dear God, please help me to have courage to stick to my commitment to following You. In all things, I want to obey You no matter what. I believe that all of Your ways are the very best ways. Amen.

OVERCOMERS, PART 1

Children, you belong to God, and you have defeated these enemies. God's Spirit is in you and is more powerful than the one that is in the world. These enemies belong to this world, and the world listens to them, because they speak its language. We belong to God.
1 JOHN 4:4–6 CEV

♡♡

Have you ever heard a friend or classmate try to brag that they're never afraid of anything? Right away, their nose should grow a little longer, like Pinocchio's, because there is *no way* that's true. Every person gets scared or anxious or worried about something some of the time. You could politely and respectfully say to anyone who denies that, "Well if you're never scared, then that means you're never brave." Read on to the next devo to find out more.

Dear God, please help me always to be honest about my fears. If I admit them, that's the first way to start overcoming them. Amen.

OVERCOMERS, PART 2

Do not be overcome by evil,
but overcome evil with good.
ROMANS 12:21 ESV

♡♡

Being brave and having courage means admitting fears and worries and facing them anyway. So you can't be brave unless you first know that you were scared of something but then dealt with it. And sometimes you deal with things so well that you totally overcome them so that they are never a fear or worry again! With God's Holy Spirit working in you to help, you can face anything and overcome it. Jesus said, "I have told you these things, so that in me you may have peace. In this world you will have trouble. But take heart! I have overcome the world" (John 16:33 NIV).

....

Dear God, I admit my fears and worries, and I admit how
much I need Your help with them. I believe with all my
heart that You can help me overcome them. Amen.

LOOK UP!

I lift up my eyes to the mountains—where
does my help come from? My help comes
*from the L*ORD*, the Maker of heaven and earth.*
PSALM 121:1–2 NIV

When you are feeling scared and unsure because you need help, what do you do? First ask the adults in your life who take care of you. That's looking up to the grown-ups! God's Word says to look up, as if to high mountains, and remember that your help comes from the Lord, "the Maker of heaven and earth"! Every bit of help from the adults in your life is ultimately because God is working through them to love and care for You! He provides anything you need with exactly the right people and resources at exactly the right time. This psalm goes on to say, "He will not let your foot slip—he who watches over you will not slumber. . . . The LORD will keep you from all harm—he will watch over your life; the LORD will watch over your coming and going both now and forevermore" (Psalm 121:3, 7–8).

Dear God, thank You that I can look up
and pray and get help from You! Amen.

NOT A CHANCE

God is love. . . . There is no fear in love.
1 JOHN 4:16, 18 NIV

♡♡

My daughters, Jodi and Lilly, recently danced on the dance worship team at our church to the song "Stand in Your Love." The song is about how fear has no power when we're standing in the love of Christ. Ever since, we've heard that song multiple times on the radio, sometimes exactly when we needed extra encouragement. God loves to remind us that truly, when we stand in His love, fear doesn't stand a chance. He is so good to us, has promised so much, and has proven Himself time and time again, so there is no reason to give in to worry and fear. The apostle John tells us that God is love and that His perfect love drives out fear.

....

Dear God, I stand in Your love. Thank You for being love itself. Thank You for Jesus, whom You sent to show us Your ultimate act of love—that You would even die to save us from sin and give us forever life with You! Nothing can take that from me, so I have no reason ever to fear a thing. Amen.

OUT OF EGYPT, PART 1

*God called to him from inside the bush, saying,
"Moses, Moses!" Moses answered, "Here I am."*
EXODUS 3:4 NLV

♡♡

Moses was an Israelite who grew up in Egypt in the king's palace because the princess had rescued him from the Nile River when he was a baby. But as a young man, Moses had run away to another country. Then God called Moses back to Egypt to lead the Israelites out of slavery and into freedom.

Moses had a lot of fear about what God wanted him to do, so God sent Moses' brother Aaron to help. God also gave Moses a shepherd's staff to perform amazing miracles. Moses and Aaron went to Pharaoh and told him that the God of Israel said, "Let My people go!" But Pharaoh refused and was even crueler to the Israelites. Finally, God told Moses and Aaron to use the special staff He had given them to bring plagues on the Egyptian people as punishment for keeping the Israelites in slavery. Finally, after many plagues, Pharaoh listened and let God's people go.

. . . .

*Dear God, thank You that You provide other people
and the right tools to help us do the brave things
You call us to do like You did for Moses. Amen.*

OUT OF EGYPT, PART 2

Moses said to the people, "Do not be afraid!
Be strong, and see how the Lord will save you today."
EXODUS 14:13 NLV

♡ ♡

As Moses led the Israelites to flee from Egypt, God led them with a huge cloud in the sky during the day and fire in the sky at night. Meanwhile, back in Egypt, Pharaoh changed his mind and sent his armies out to capture the Israelites again. The Egyptians caught up with the Israelites at the Red Sea, and God's people seemed totally trapped. But God had an amazing plan. Moses stretched his hand toward the sea, and God pushed the water back and made a path of dry land through the Red Sea! The Israelites followed the path, with huge walls of water rising up on either side of them. As the Egyptians chased the Israelites, God made the waters crash down to kill the Egyptians, but He kept the Israelites safe. Just as He had promised, God made a miraculous way to bring His people out of slavery and into freedom.

....

Dear God, when I'm not sure where to go, please lead me like You led the Israelites with a cloud in the sky by day and fire in the sky by night. And like You parted the Red Sea, show me how You will help me get through what seems totally impossible too! Amen.

HOLD YOUR HEAD HIGH

*The LORD will be your confidence and will
keep your foot from being caught.*
PROVERBS 3:26 ESV

We've all done things that are embarrassing or awkward, things that turn our face red and make us want to melt into the floor or become invisible. And after it's over, the weirdness can live on in our minds for a long time later. But it's usually much bigger in our own minds than in the minds of others. Yes, whoever was watching might remember for a while. You might even get teased a little. But that shows others' character, not yours. You can choose to show strong character and courage by not forgetting that *everyone* has embarrassing moments. So let it roll right off your back. Hold your head high, remembering you are a child of the one true God who loves you and is always looking out for you no matter what embarrassing things you do.

*Dear God, please comfort me when I'm embarrassed.
Help me remember that You are my confidence.
Thank You for loving me no matter what. Amen.*

CAN'T STOP, WON'T STOP, PART 1

Don't worry about anything, but pray about everything.
With thankful hearts, offer up your prayers and
requests to God. Then, because you belong to Christ
Jesus, God will bless you with peace that no one
can completely understand. And this peace
will control the way you think and feel.
PHILIPPIANS 4:6–7 CEV

♡♡

It's mind-blowing that the God of the universe wants you to talk to Him all the time. His Word tells us again and again to keep on praying to Him for everything, at all times. It literally says, "Never stop praying" (1 Thessalonians 5:17 NLT). You can make this your motto about prayer: "Can't stop, won't stop!"

....

Dear God, I'm so grateful You want me to pray
to You and never stop for any reason. It's such
a gift that You are always with me, always
listening to me. I love You, Lord! Amen.

CAN'T STOP, WON'T STOP, PART 2

Never stop praying, especially for others.
Always pray by the power of the Spirit.
Stay alert and keep praying for God's people.
EPHESIANS 6:18 CEV

♡♡

As you pray every day, all the time, you build your courage, because praying reminds you of who is always right there with you. Prayer is never just talking to yourself or to some god who doesn't care. Prayer is a direct line of communication with the King of all kings and Lord of all lords! Wow! He loves you enough that He sent His only Son, Jesus, to die to save you. He wants to empower you with great courage and faith in Him for whatever you're facing!

....

Dear God, please keep reminding me every single moment that You are with me and You want me to talk to You about anything and everything! It's a huge honor that You love to hear from me! Amen.

TWO BRAVE SPIES,
PART 1

They told Moses, "We went to the land where you
sent us. It does flow with milk and honey. This is
its fruit. But the people who live in the land are
strong. The cities have walls and are very large."
NUMBERS 13:27–28 NLV

Do you know the story of Joshua and Caleb in the
Bible? Moses sent them to see what the land of Canaan was like because God had said to Moses that He
was one day soon going to give it to His people. So
Joshua, Caleb, and ten other men went to spy on the
land of Canaan for forty days. When they returned,
they reported that the land was wonderful but the
people were very powerful and the cities were well
protected. Joshua and Caleb weren't scared though.

Dear God, help me to be like Joshua and Caleb—
not scared of things against me that might seem big
and powerful, because I know You are with me! Amen.

TWO BRAVE SPIES, PART 2

*[Joshua and Caleb] said to all the people of Israel,
"The land we passed through to spy out is a very good
land. If the Lord is pleased with us, then He will bring
us into this land and give it to us. It is a land which
flows with milk and honey. Only do not go against the
Lord. And do not be afraid of the people of the land."*
NUMBERS 14:7–9 NLV

♡♡

Joshua and Caleb weren't scared because they were
confident that with God's help they could still take
over the land of Canaan. But ten of the spies said that
it would be way too hard. Then those ten men spread
so much fear among the people of Israel about Canaan that the people rebelled and complained against
their leaders, Moses and Aaron. God grew angry
with the people of Israel because they listened to
fear rather than listening to the courage and faith of
Joshua and Caleb.

....

*Dear God, help me not to listen to fears that some
people spread that say You are not powerful enough or
in control to work out Your good plans. I trust in You,
and I know You can accomplish anything! Amen.*

POWERFUL PEP TALK

*Be strong and brave! Be careful to do everything
my servant Moses taught you. Never stop reading The
Book of the Law he gave you. Day and night you must
think about what it says. If you obey it completely,
you and Israel will be able to take this land. I've
commanded you to be strong and brave. Don't ever
be afraid or discouraged! I am the Lord your God,
and I will be there to help you wherever you go.*
JOSHUA 1:8–9 CEV

♡♡

God called Joshua to be the one who would lead
His people into the promised land after wandering in
the desert for forty years. In Joshua 1 you can read
the powerful pep talk God gave Joshua to help him
be the brave new leader. It's not just for Joshua
though. You can read this scripture and let God
powerfully pep talk you as well, as He leads you into
the wonderful purposes He has for your life!

*Dear God, thank You for Your powerful pep talk to
Joshua long ago, and that I can be strengthened and
encouraged by those same words even now. Amen.*

WONDERING WHY,
PART 1

*What we are suffering now cannot compare
with the glory that will be shown to us.*
ROMANS 8:18 CEV

Sometimes when we're scared, God does not just suddenly fix things like we hope. We sure wish He would, and we pray and cry to Him, asking Him to see our fears and our needs and make everything all okay right away. And when He doesn't, our trust in Him can really be shaken as we wonder why. I've lived through that and have asked God many questions. I have even held on to anger and blame toward Him at times—but that's not good.

....

*Dear God, please forgive me for holding on to anger at
You. Give me courage to keep trusting You even when
I'm confused about why You don't fix things as I want
You to. Please hold me tight when I'm hurting. Amen.*

WONDERING WHY, PART 2

*You will suffer for a while, but God will make
you complete, steady, strong, and firm.
God will be in control forever!*
1 Peter 5:10–11 CEV

Even when I'm confused and hurting and frustrated over a prayer that seems to go unanswered, I've seen God answer other prayers and show His love in many other ways at the same time. And so I have learned to continue to trust even through awfully sad and scary times. I can't possibly see all the good things God is doing even when life seems hard, but one day in heaven I will understand. Then God will make all things perfect and new. You know how it is to trust that something works but not know exactly *how* it works, and you can trust God even more!

....

*Dear God, when I don't see You answering my prayers as I
hope You will, please let me see how You are providing
in other ways and constantly caring for me. Amen.*

BRAVE AND READY FOR GOD'S GOOD PLANS

"For I know the plans I have for you," says the LORD.
"They are plans for good and not for disaster,
to give you a future and a hope."
JEREMIAH 29:11 NLT

♡♡

My daughter Lilly recently had a guest speaker in her class who is a meteorologist. He talked about how he used to love to chase storms. There is no way I'd want to do that, but I don't see that as a fear I need to get over. Not everyone needs to chase storms, certainly not me! But I'm glad some people find them fascinating. Why? Because that means they can learn from them and help protect people from them. It's so cool how God gives different interests and talents to different people, and how He helps people to be brave for exactly the good plans He has for them to do.

. . . .

Dear God, I believe You have wonderful plans for my
life and will help me have the courage and ability to
do them exactly when I need to. Guide me in Your
will and grow me in great faith in You! Amen.

RAHAB'S COURAGE, PART 1

*[Joshua] said to them, "Go and spy out
the land, and Jericho." So they went
and came to the house of Rahab.*
JOSHUA 2:1 NLV

Do you know the story of Rahab in the Bible? She helped two men whom Joshua (the leader of the Israelite people after Moses died) sent into the land of Canaan to spy on the city of Jericho. The men came to her house, but then someone found out and warned the king that they were spies. So Rahab helped the two spies hide to protect them. And before the spies went to sleep for the night, Rahab went up to them on her roof to say that she trusted in their God and asked them to help protect her family when they came into the land of Canaan to take it over.

. . . .

*Dear God, please give me courage like
Rahab had to help protect people
when You need me to! Amen.*

RAHAB'S COURAGE,
PART 2

"Bring out the woman and all who are with her, as you promised her." So the young men who had spied out the land went in, and brought out Rahab and her father and mother and brothers and all she had. They brought out all of her family and took them outside the tents of Israel.
JOSHUA 6:22–23 NLV

♡♡

The spies promised to help protect Rahab and her family as long as she did not tell anyone about their plans. Then Rahab let them down by a rope through the window and told them to hide for three days in the hill country before returning home. And later, by that same red rope, the spies knew where to find her and her family to protect them when the Israelites took over Jericho. The Israelite spies had needed help, and God provided Rahab to believe in Him and have courage to hide the spies at exactly the right time.

....

Dear God, please help me to remember that You provide exactly the right help at exactly the right time. Amen.

DON'T LET COURAGE MELT AWAY

The Israelites were paralyzed with fear at this
turn of events, and their courage melted away.
JOSHUA 7:5 NLT

It's good when snow and ice melt away when it means spring is coming. It's good to melt chocolate when you're making yummy candy treats! But this scripture says the courage of God's people melted away, and that's *not* good! We never want that to happen to us, and if it does for some reason, we need to figure out how to get it back solid again! We can take a good lesson from the story this scripture comes from. You can read the whole story in Joshua 7, but basically the Israelites had disobeyed God and He let them be defeated in battle as their consequences. If we disobey God, He is not going to fill us with His good courage either.

Dear God, please help me to keep obeying You and
Your Word and to quickly ask for forgiveness and make
things right when I make mistakes. I want to keep Your
courage in me. I don't want it to melt away! Amen.

COURAGE FOR HOMESICKNESS

*God has said, "I will never leave
you or let you be alone."*
HEBREWS 13:5 NLV

♡♡

Have you ever felt horribly homesick? I remember that feeling at camp in middle school, and I remember it when I first moved to college. It takes a lot of courage to fight through the feelings of homesickness to have a good experience when you're missing home and family. Remember this promise in Hebrews 13:5—God is with you constantly and will never let you be alone. In times when you aren't in the places you love most with the people you love most, let God show you how He will send His love and comfort to you in other ways and through other people—and hopefully you will even come to love the new place and experience. I soon got over my homesickness at college, and I loved my time there *so* much! Stay close to God through prayer and reading His Word and in total trust that His Holy Spirit is inside you and knows everything you think and say and do. God cares about you like no one else does!

Dear God, when I'm feeling homesick, please make me brave to learn and grow from the experience. Amen.

A MIGHTY HERO

The angel of the LORD appeared to [Gideon]
and said, "Mighty hero, the LORD is with you!"
JUDGES 6:12 NLT

♡♡

Think of a person you really look up to. How does it make you feel if they give you a wonderful compliment? Pretty awesome, right? So imagine how Gideon must have felt when God spoke to him through an angel's appearance and called him a "mighty hero." Wow!

You can think of God telling you the same thing He told Gideon. You are totally capable of being a mighty hero for God. He is with you, constantly giving you courage and power. Those qualities don't come from yourself but from God's Holy Spirit in you.

. . . .

Dear God, I trust that You are with me in everything
I do. I want to be a mighty hero who points other
people to You and Your love! Amen.

GIDEON'S COURAGE

The LORD turned to [Gideon] and said,
"Go with the strength you have, and rescue
Israel from the Midianites. I am sending you!"
JUDGES 6:14 NLT

♡♡

Gideon was filled with powerful faith, and the Lord kept speaking to him to show him how to defeat Israel's enemy, the Midianites.

Gideon started with an army of 32,000 men, but 22,000 left. They were too scared to fight. Then God told Gideon He wanted only 300 men to fight against the powerful Midianites, to prove that all the real power came from God alone. So, with God's power, Gideon and the army of only 300 men rescued Israel from Midian.

Gideon was just an ordinary man doing ordinary things—in the beginning. But by trusting God and growing in faith, Gideon went on to do *extraordinary* things.

....

Dear God, even when I see lots of people giving
up all around me, like Gideon saw, please help
me bravely remember that You can use anyone
and anything, no matter how big or small,
to accomplish Your good plans. Amen.

COURAGE IN THE SADDEST TIMES

Those who have sorrow are happy,
because they will be comforted.
MATTHEW 5:4 NLV

♡♡

Moving forward when you've lost a close loved one and have to figure out how to do life without them takes a great amount of courage. Maybe you know what this is like. Our family knows this firsthand, and it's hard to have courage when grieving. If you know your loved one knew Jesus as Savior, then you can be confident that he or she is in heaven with God. And with Jesus as your Savior, God is with you through the Holy Spirit. So there is super big comfort and courage in knowing that God is with your loved one and God is with you. So, in a way, you are not that far apart at all! I know it's awful not to talk with or hug your loved one who has died, but you can always pray like this:

....

Dear God, I miss my loved one so much. Please tell
them that and hug them for me. Please show them
the cool things I am doing here in this life, and thank
You for the confident hope of forever life You give
everyone who trusts in Jesus as Savior. Amen.

HEART OF A LION

*The sinful run away when no one is trying to
catch them, but those who are right with God
have as much strength of heart as a lion.*
PROVERBS 28:1 NLV

This scripture is comparing people who don't trust
Jesus as Savior with people who do. If you are right
with God, meaning you have asked Jesus to be your
Savior, this scripture tells you that you are as bold and
brave as a lion! That's pretty amazing. And people who
don't trust Jesus as Savior are often so afraid of any
little thing that they're even running when there is
no danger. They might not ever admit that, but deep
down they have no faith to give them courage. But
everyone who trusts Jesus as Savior does have faith.
They are right with God because of Jesus and so are
able to be as courageous as the mightiest lion.

*Dear Jesus, I trust You, and I know You make me
right with God. I have nothing to fear. My heart
is brave and strong because of You! Amen.*

WHEN FRIENDS MOVE AWAY

Two people are better off than one, for they can help each other succeed. If one person falls, the other can reach out and help. But someone who falls alone is in real trouble.
ECCLESIASTES 4:9–10 NLT

When I was in the first grade, my best friend had to move away. We were young and didn't have a good way of keeping in touch, so I've never talked to her again. I remember being so bummed. Thankfully, these days it's easier to keep in touch with friends even after a move, but still friendship does change when you're apart. To lose closeness with a friend might make you too sad and scared to reach out and make more friends, but don't give in to that fear. Ask God to help bring a new good friend or two into your life. He will answer and provide who you need when you wait patiently on Him! He knows friendship and encouragement are important.

. . . .

Dear God, please comfort me when I'm sad and missing a friend who has moved away. Please help us keep in touch, and please bring both of us new friends to enjoy life with. Amen.

COURAGE TO CRY

Then Jesus cried.
JOHN 11:35 NLV

Do you ever feel like crying and you're not sure why? I totally get that! In fact, right now as I write this, I feel that way. I think I want to cry because of frustration and sadness, and I think it's brave to stop and give myself time and space to feel those emotions and give them to God in prayer. I have learned that if I bottle up my emotions, they often explode in other ways or make me feel sick inside. So, don't ever think that crying just means you're wimpy or babyish. Listening to and figuring out where your emotions are coming from and giving them time and space to release actually takes a lot of courage. When you can name your emotions and realize the source of them, they don't have to scare you or make you act out in ways that might get you in trouble. Telling God and trusted grown-ups who care all about them are some of the very best ways to deal with them.

. . . .

Dear God, give me wisdom about having courage to cry. Help me to listen to my emotions and figure out how to handle them in healthy ways. Amen.

COURAGE TO LOOK AWAY

I will set no sinful thing in front of my eyes.
PSALM 101:3 NLV

It seems like the whole world spends huge amounts of time online and on their phones these days. Having access to so much information and cool ways to interact with people is great, but there is a whole lot of junk online too. You constantly need to ask God for wisdom and listen to good and healthy rules for setting limits with it. We all do, grown-ups like me too. You also need to have courage to look away and do something else if friends are pressuring you to spend time online in ways you know are wrong or have been told are off-limits by your parents. This can be hard, especially when it feels like so many others have no limits online. But stay strong and keep courage. There are many good things to do instead!

Dear God, please help me to have courage to set limits and look away from unhealthy things online. The world is connected through the internet, but I need to disconnect in healthy ways too. Amen.

RUTH'S COURAGE, PART 1

*Ruth replied, "Don't ask me to
leave you and turn back."*
RUTH 1:16 NLT

♡♡

Do you know the story of Ruth in the Bible? About ten years after she got married, her husband died, and so did his brother and father. So, of the family, only Ruth, her mother-in-law, Naomi, and her sister-in-law, Orpah, were left. They were in a terrible situation. It was hard for women alone to find good work, enough food, and a safe place to live.

Naomi told Ruth and Orpah to leave her and go back to their old homes, for they were still young and could find new husbands. So Orpah decided to leave and kissed her mother-in-law goodbye. But Ruth refused. She clung to Naomi, saying, "Please don't ask me to leave you! I want to go where you go. I want to stay where you stay. I want your people to be my people. I want your God to be my God. I never want to leave you as long as I am alive."

....

Dear God, please give me courage to be loyal to loved ones like Ruth was, even during hard times. Help me to look out not only for myself but for others too. Amen.

RUTH'S COURAGE, PART 2

*When Naomi saw that Ruth was determined
to go with her, she said nothing more.*
RUTH 1:18 NLT

When Naomi realized Ruth's great and loyal love for her, she stopped pushing her to go. The two traveled together back to Bethlehem. There God blessed Ruth as she worked picking up leftover grain in the fields. God led her to the fields owned by a kind and good man named Boaz. When Boaz heard about Ruth's loyalty and love for her mother-in-law, he was impressed, and he admired her. He protected and provided for Ruth and Naomi and grew to love Ruth.

....

*Dear God, help me to remember Ruth's story and
how You love to bless people for being brave and
loyal. Please show me the people in my life whom
You always want me to be loyal to. Amen.*

FINDING A MATCH,
PART 1

In his grace, God has given us different
gifts for doing certain things well.
ROMANS 12:6 NLT

♡♡

Do you play any musical instruments? I took eight years of piano lessons when I was young. I enjoyed playing in my living room just for fun, but I also could have practiced a whole lot more. (Maybe you can relate! Ha!) I did okay but not great even when I did practice a lot. And I *never* got over my shaky-finger fear of piano recitals! I definitely could have used more courage! I'm glad I took piano, because learning and loving music is so good for the brain. But I wish I hadn't stressed it so much. And looking back, I've realized how good it is to figure out the things that don't match up with the talents and gifts we've been given.

. . . .

Dear God, please help me to realize what the good
gifts are that You've given me for doing things well.
Help me to learn and grow and improve my brain,
learning from both success and failure every day! Amen.

FINDING A MATCH, PART 2

There are different kinds of gifts. But it is the same Holy Spirit Who gives them. There are different kinds of work to be done for Him. But the work is for the same Lord. There are different ways of doing His work. But it is the same God who uses all these ways in all people. The Holy Spirit works in each person in one way or another for the good of all.
1 CORINTHIANS 12:4–7 NLV

It's okay that piano didn't come easily to me. Trying something new and giving it your best shot takes courage and then sometimes even more courage to admit it's just not your thing. Then you can move on to something new, with gratitude for the learning experience, and ask God to help you keep learning what does and does not match up with the gifts and talents He has given you.

....

Dear God, please help me to be brave enough to try new things and brave and wise enough to know when to let them go or when to pursue them more. Amen.

KEEP MOVING

Use your body to honor God.
1 Corinthians 6:20 CEV

♡♡

Volleyball was another thing I tried when I was young that I wasn't any good at, even though I'm tall so people expected me to be good. Well, they were wrong! You might love playing sports or you'd rather just watch them or you want nothing to do with them at all. And whatever the case, that's okay! What's important is finding ways to keep your body moving and healthy. The older you get, this can be harder to do, so start great habits now while you're young that will hopefully stick with you forever. Even if sports aren't your thing or you feel like you don't have much athletic ability or coordination, be brave enough to keep trying until you find the physical activities that you do enjoy enough to make a habit of them. Regular exercise affects your brain in many good and healthy ways and helps give you confidence and courage for everything you do!

....

Dear God, thank You for the body You've given me. I want to take care of it well. Please help me to keep it healthy with good exercise and activities. Amen.

DAVID AND GOLIATH, PART 1

*Goliath, the Philistine champion from Gath,
came out from the Philistine ranks. Then David
heard him shout his usual taunt to the army of Israel.*
1 SAMUEL 17:23 NLT

For many days on a battlefield, the evil Philistine Goliath, a giant of a man, was teasing and taunting God's people. He dared anyone to try to defeat him. This went on for forty days and forty nights, with not one man from the Israelite army willing to fight Goliath. He was too big, and they were too scared. When the young shepherd David witnessed this, he was not afraid of Goliath, and he offered to fight. King Saul scoffed at the idea. But David said, "I kill lions and bears that attack my sheep. God protects me from them, and He will protect me as I fight Goliath."

David prepared himself for battle with only his shepherd's staff, his sling, and five smooth stones. Then he started across the valley to confront Goliath. . . .

*Dear God, help me to have the kind of fearless
confidence in You that David had! Amen.*

DAVID AND GOLIATH, PART 2

"Don't worry about this Philistine,"
David told Saul. "I'll go fight him!"
1 SAMUEL 17:32 NLT

♡ ♡

Sneering, Goliath said to David, "Do you think I'm just a dog, since you're coming at me with only a stick?"

David replied to the giant, "You come to me with sword and spear to kill me, but I come to you in the name of the Lord Almighty, the God of Israel. You have defied Him, but today He will conquer you! Everyone here will know that the Lord rescues His people—but not with sword and spear. This is God's battle, and He will give you to us!"

David loaded his sling and launched one smooth stone at Goliath. The stone sailed through the air and struck the giant hard, right in the middle of his forehead. Goliath stumbled and fell facedown. Then David ran to grab Goliath's sword, and he used it to kill the giant and cut off his head. When the Philistines saw their strongest man was dead, they all ran away, while the Israelite army shouted in victory and chased after them.

....

Dear God, thank You for the big win for David over Goliath. Remind me every day that You can help me have victory over any giant problems in my life too. Amen.

A BRAVE AND LOYAL FRIEND, PART 1

There was an immediate bond between them, for Jonathan loved David.
1 SAMUEL 18:1 NLT

After David bravely killed the giant Goliath, Saul, who was king of Israel, was super impressed. So King Saul summoned David to work for him, and David soon met the king's son, Jonathan. In no time the two young men had an extra-special bond. Jonathan loved David and promised to be his loyal friend forever.

Since David was such a brave young man, King Saul wanted David to lead his armies. And because God was with him, David succeeded in all he did. But then one day King Saul grew jealous that maybe the people of Israel respected David more than they respected him. The king grew so jealous that he no longer trusted David and actually wanted to kill him! He told all his servants and even his son Jonathan to kill David. But never could Jonathan kill his best friend, David. Instead, he warned David about the king's orders.

Dear God, help me to be brave like Jonathan and protect my friends from evil. Amen.

A BRAVE AND LOYAL FRIEND, PART 2

"Tell me what I can do to help you," Jonathan exclaimed.
1 SAMUEL 20:4 NLT

♡♡

Jonathan helped protect David. Then he defended David by reminding his father, "David has never done any wrong to you. He has only helped you! Remember how he killed Goliath? Why would you now want to kill David, an innocent man, for no reason at all?" Jonathan convinced King Saul to trust David again.

But it didn't take long for King Saul to grow jealous once again and think evil thoughts toward David. He attacked David. And Jonathan risked his own life to protect and help David in every way he could, despite King Saul's anger. Jonathan knew his father's plans were wrong, and he would stay loyal to David no matter what.

Jonathan could have become jealous of David. He could have wanted to become the next king after Saul instead of David. But Jonathan loved God and loved his friend David.

....

Dear God, please help me to be the kind of friend that Jonathan was—courageous and loyal and loving and selfless no matter what. Amen.

TRAPPED

Fearing people is a dangerous trap,
but trusting the LORD means safety.
PROVERBS 29:25 NLT

♡♡

Think about a time when you felt trapped. Maybe you were actually locked in somewhere and couldn't get out. Or your hand was trapped in the car door. I've been there, done that! Ouch! Or maybe it's more of feeling stuck in a situation, like there's no end to the stress you're feeling. I've been there, done that too. Ugh! It can be super scary and/or super stressful to feel stuck somewhere and not know how to get out. Proverbs 29:25 talks about how fearing people is a dangerous trap. We can get our minds stuck in a rut that feels hopeless to get out of if we constantly fear other people. Trusting God is where our safety is. He is in control over all things and all people, and when we trust Him completely over everything else, He provides us with ultimate safety.

Dear God, I want to only fear You, meaning I respect
You, and I don't want to fear any other people or
any hard situations. When I trust in You completely,
I know You will keep me safe. Amen.

HOLDING YOU UP

Don't be afraid, for I am with you. Don't be discouraged,
for I am your God. I will strengthen you and help you.
I will hold you up with my victorious right hand.
ISAIAH 41:10 NLT

Have you ever been so sick or in so much pain that you could not hold yourself up? Maybe your mom or dad had to carry you, or a friend let you lean on them. In those moments, that is God's love for you coming through in the people who are helping. When you look back and think about those hard times and who God provided to help you, you can look forward and not be afraid of anything that might happen today or in the future because You can trust that God will provide exactly the people and things you need to deal with any difficulty to come.

. . . .

Dear God, thank You for being with me and not wanting
me to be discouraged. I'm grateful for all the ways You
have strengthened me and held me up in the past, and
for Your promise to do the same in the future. Amen.

A BRAVE PROMISE, PART 1

[Hannah] gave him the name Samuel,
saying, "I have asked the Lord for him."
1 SAMUEL 1:20 NLV

A woman named Hannah in the Bible wanted to be a mother so much, but she had no children. Every year she traveled with her husband to a place called Shiloh during a celebration to worship God. And every year Hannah cried and prayed, asking God to bless her with a son. Sometimes she felt as though God had forgotten or didn't care about her. But still Hannah kept praying. She promised God, "If you give me a son, I will give him back to You for all the days of his life."

A religious leader named Eli had watched Hannah praying, and then after he talked to her, he said, "Go peacefully, and may the God of Israel give you what you have asked."

Right away Hannah felt much better. She went home with her husband, and soon she did have a baby boy! She named him Samuel, saying, "I asked the Lord for him."

....

Dear God, even if I'm feeling forgotten by You,
like Hannah did for a while, help me to keep
on bravely praying and trusting You! Amen.

A BRAVE PROMISE, PART 2

*Hannah prayed and said, "My heart is happy
in the Lord. My strength is honored in the
Lord. . . . There is no one holy like the Lord."*
1 SAMUEL 2:1–2 NLV

♡ ♡

Hannah dearly loved and cared for baby Samuel, but she never forgot her prayers and her promise to God. When the little boy was old enough, Hannah returned to Shiloh to the temple where she had met Eli. She said, "I asked for my son, and God gave him to me. So now I give him back to God for his whole life." Hannah meant she was letting Samuel live at the temple to grow up and be a servant of God there under Eli's care.

Every year Hannah came back to the temple to visit Samuel. And God blessed Hannah with three more sons and two daughters. She was greatly rewarded for being faithful to the Lord.

Samuel grew to be a very important leader and speaker for God. He was a blessing to all the people of Israel because Hannah kept her promise to God about her son.

. . . .

*Dear God, help me to be brave like Hannah
and keep my promises to You! Amen.*

BRAVELY WAITING, PART 1

Wait patiently for the LORD. Be brave and courageous. Yes, wait patiently for the LORD.
PSALM 27:14 NLT

What's your favorite amusement park ride? Big Thunder Mountain Railroad at Disney World is mine. Or maybe Rockin' Roller Coaster at Hollywood Studios. Oh, it's hard to decide! If you're in a long line waiting for a favorite amusement park ride, you don't need a lot of bravery. You're just standing there, probably really excited. And if you're in line while shopping, you're just standing there, probably really bored. But what if your family is waiting to hear if someone you love has cancer or not? Or waiting to hear about a job your dad desperately needs? Or your mom's car broke down along a busy highway and you're waiting for a tow truck to help?

....

Dear God, please let me feel You extra close to me when I am waiting during hard and stressful times and feeling impatient. I don't want worry to take over or to make bad choices during those times. Amen.

BRAVELY WAITING, PART 2

The Lord is good to those who wait for Him, to the one who looks for Him.
LAMENTATIONS 3:25 NLV

In hard times, it does take a whole lot of courage to wait. The time in between the stressful situation and the outcome is often a very scary place to be. Your mind can go a little crazy thinking of all the "what ifs" and worries if you let it. So *don't* let it. Focus on scripture like Psalm 27:14 to calm you. Continue to live life with joy in the wait times, choosing to trust that God is in control and knows exactly what is best. He never leaves you. And nothing stops His love for you. Call out to Him in times of waiting, and be patient and brave.

Dear God, I don't like to wait, sometimes because it's boring but sometimes because it's scary. In all waiting times, please pull me closer to You and help me trust You more. Amen.

THE LORD IS LIGHT

The Lord is my light and the One Who saves me.
Whom should I fear? The Lord is the strength
of my life. Of whom should I be afraid?
PSALM 27:1 NLV

One of my least favorite rides ever is Space Mountain at Magic Kingdom at Disney World. My daughters love it, but since it is pitch black for most of the ride, I am not a fan. I prefer some light so I can see what's coming on a roller coaster! Darkness does have a lot of unknown and possibly hidden dangers, and that's often why it can be scary. So I love this scripture that says God is our light. We don't have to worry about the unknown because He knows it, and He saves us from any hidden dangers. We have nothing to fear with the Lord as our light, our Savior, and our strength.

....

Dear God, thank You that You are light, and You are
my light. There is no darkness with You and nothing
is hidden from or unknown by You. You save me and
give me strength and courage so that I don't
have to fear anyone or anything. Amen.

HIGH WAY OF WISDOM

"Give me an understanding heart so that I can govern your people well and know the difference between right and wrong. For who by himself is able to govern this great people of yours?" The Lord was pleased that Solomon had asked for wisdom.
1 KINGS 3:9–10 NLT

Do you know the story of King Solomon in the Bible who could ask God for anything but he asked God for wisdom? That was very brave of him! Solomon loved God and knew wisdom would be most valuable—because wanting to follow God's ways of right and wrong and lead others in them matters forever, not just for a little while like the things of this world. It takes great courage to be someone who thinks about the things of heaven more than the things of earth (Colossians 3:2).

You can have great courage like Solomon too. Every time you find yourself faced with a choice either to focus on the things of the world or to focus on God's wise ways of right and wrong, choose the high way!

Dear God, remind me every day of the story of King Solomon. Help me to ask You for wisdom like he did. Amen.

SOAKED WITH WISDOM

*If any of you lacks wisdom, you should ask God,
who gives generously to all without finding fault, and it
will be given to you. But when you ask, you must believe
and not doubt, because the one who doubts is like a
wave of the sea, blown and tossed by the wind.*
JAMES 1:5–6 NIV

When you do ask God for wisdom, you need to be
brave and not doubt that He will give it to you. And
the Bible says He gives it generously, not like just a
little sprinkle of it but more like the end of a really
great waterslide splash super-soaking you! So believe that truth and then ask God to help you use that
wisdom in every single area of your life—at home,
with family, at school, with friends, during sports
and activities, when using social media, and on and
on. Don't let people who don't love God make you
second-guess the wisdom of the Bible and the wisdom God gives through the power of the Holy Spirit
working in you.

*Dear God, I believe in You and Your Word and that
Your ways of right and wrong are wisest and best.
Please keep on giving and help me keep on
using Your great wisdom. Amen.*

FOR SUCH A TIME AS THIS, PART 1

*[Esther] found favor and kindness with him more than
all the young women, so that he set the queen's crown
on her head and made her queen instead of Vashti.*
ESTHER 2:17 NLV

King Xerxes of Persia began searching for a new
queen, he liked Esther best. She was a Jewish woman,
but she had kept her family history a secret. Meanwhile, a man named Haman was given a high royal
position. Haman wanted all people to bow down and
honor him. Esther's cousin Mordecai refused to bow
down to anyone but God. Because of this, Haman
was filled with hate for Jewish people, and he convinced King Xerxes to order a decree to have them all
killed. Mordecai got word to Esther about what was
going on.

*Dear God, remind me of Esther's story and that You
sometimes call ordinary people to great positions
like Queen Esther. But even if I always live a very
ordinary life, I want to be grateful and brave
in anything You ask me to do. Amen.*

FOR SUCH A TIME AS THIS, PART 2

*"Who knows if perhaps you were made
queen for just such a time as this?"*
ESTHER 4:14 NLT

Mordecai urged Esther to go to the king and beg for mercy for the Jewish people. But Esther said, "If I go to the king without being invited, I will be killed. The only exception is if the king extends his scepter and spares my life." And Mordecai said, "If you are silent, help will come to the Jews from another way, but you and your father's family will die. So who knows but maybe you became queen to help at exactly a time like this!"

So Esther went to the king, and he did not turn her away but held out his scepter and welcomed her. Her life was spared, and because of her faith and courage, she allowed God to work through her to save her entire nation of people.

*Dear God, help me to grow up to be as
faithful and courageous as Esther! Amen.*

TROUBLE = JOY?
PART 1

*Dear brothers and sisters, when troubles
of any kind come your way, consider it
an opportunity for great joy.*
JAMES 1:2 NLT

God's Word is sure not always easy to read. If anyone
ever tries to tell you it's just a warm, fuzzy book that
always makes you feel good, they are big-time wrong.
Take James 1:2 for example. Seriously? I don't know
about you, but when I first think of great joy, I think
of fun things like winning a game or playing with a
puppy or going on a great vacation with family to the
beach or an amusement park. I don't usually think of
troubles bringing great joy!

*Dear God, help me to remember that Your Word
doesn't always just comfort me or make me feel
better about myself. It's meant to change me and
help me grow and be better and braver because
I trust in You more and more! Amen.*

TROUBLE = JOY?
PART 2

*For you know that when your faith is tested,
your endurance has a chance to grow. So let it grow,
for when your endurance is fully developed, you will
be perfect and complete, needing nothing.*
JAMES 1:3–4 NLT

♡♡

When God allows tests or trouble to come your way, He is giving you a chance to learn how to trust Him more and get stronger and stronger in your faith until it's totally complete! Think of how brave you'll be then! Can you think of a time when you got through something really hard, and when you looked back you realized how the tough experience helped you to become tougher?

....

*Dear God, help me to think about troubles in a
different kind of way than I usually do. I want to
see them as a chance to grow closer to You
and stronger and braver in You! Amen.*

SAVED FROM FEARS

Honor the LORD with me! Celebrate his great name.
I asked the LORD for help, and he saved me from
all my fears. Keep your eyes on the LORD!
PSALM 34:3–5 CEV

People who have been in bad car accidents are likely to struggle with fear of driving. People who have been bitten by dogs are likely to have a fear of dogs. People who have had close calls with tornadoes or hurricanes are likely to be more scared of bad weather in the future. No doubt, our scary experiences in the past create some of the fears we have. But God knows each of us individually very well. He knows all about every hard thing we've ever been through. He knows every detail about us, down to the very number of hairs on our head! So we can admit each fear and let Him take them from us and fill us instead with His peace!

....

Dear God, You know exactly the reasons I struggle
with certain kinds of fears. Please comfort and
encourage in the specific ways I need in
order to overcome my fears. Amen.

DON'T LIVE IN FEAR, PART 1

*You are standing under the powerful hand of God.
At the right time He will lift you up. Give all your
worries to Him because He cares for you.*
1 Peter 5:6–7 NLV

♡♡

When we have scary experiences, we naturally want to avoid the possibility of anything similar happening ever again. For example, I was attacked by a huge dog once, and even though I *love* dogs, right afterward I felt like I might never want to be anywhere near any large dog except my own ever again. But did that mean I should never go to a public park or beach again where large dogs often are, or the house of any friend who had a large dog? Living in fear like that wouldn't be healthy. If at all possible, it's best to work through fears created from our experiences and not let them overcome us or keep us from doing good things.

....

Dear God, thank You that You care about my fears. Please help me to want to work through them and learn from them rather than to run away from and avoid them. Amen.

DON'T LIVE IN FEAR, PART 2

For the LORD God is our sun and our shield. He gives us grace and glory. The LORD will withhold no good thing from those who do what is right. O LORD of Heaven's Armies, what joy for those who trust in you.
PSALM 84:11–12 NLT

♡♡

Depending on what our fears are, sometimes we can work them out with help from Mom and Dad and/or other family and friends, and sometimes we need extra help, like seeing a good counselor for therapy. God is always able to provide exactly the comfort and the people and the resources we need to help us with anxiety and fear. He loves to shine on us and protect us in all kinds of ways, just like Psalm 84 says. Just ask Him and trust Him!

. . . .

Dear God, please help me with my worries and fear. Give me comfort and wisdom and provide everything I need, including the right people and resources, to overcome them. Thank You! Amen.

THREE BRAVE FRIENDS, PART 1

*"Shadrach, Meshach, and Abednego. . .pay no attention
to you, Your Majesty. They refuse to serve your gods
and do not worship the gold statue you have set up."*
DANIEL 3:12 NLT

♡♡

After King Nebuchadnezzar of Babylon took over
Jerusalem, he decided to have a gold statue built to
look like a god and ordered everyone to worship it.
Anyone who did not would be thrown into a fiery
furnace. But three Israelite men named Shadrach,
Meshach, and Abednego refused to worship anyone
but the one true God. So some men went to the king
and tattled on them for not bowing down. This made
King Nebuchadnezzar furious. "Is this true?" he asked
them. "I will give you one more chance to obey me,
and if not, you will be thrown into the fiery furnace.
Who will be able to rescue you then?"

Shadrach, Meshach, and Abednego bravely said,
"If you throw us into the fiery furnace, the God we
serve is able to save us from it. But even if He does
not, we will *never* serve your gods."

....

*Dear God, help me to have the kind of courage
that Shadrach, Meschach, and Abednego had.
They knew that even dying for You was better
than worshipping a false god. Amen.*

THREE BRAVE FRIENDS, PART 2

If we are thrown into the blazing furnace,
the God whom we serve is able to save us.
He will rescue us from your power, Your Majesty.
DANIEL 3:17 NLT

The angry king ordered the furnace to be seven times hotter than normal. He commanded some of his strongest soldiers to tie up Shadrach, Meshach, and Abednego and throw them into the fire. The flames were blazing so hot that the soldiers were killed as they threw the three friends in.

As King Nebuchadnezzar was watching all this, suddenly he leaped to his feet. "Look!" he said. "I see *four* men walking around in the fire, untied and unharmed, and the fourth man looks like a god!" So he called for the men to come out of the fire—and they did! Not even a hair on their heads was burned, and they didn't even smell like fire!

The king said, "Praise to the God of Shadrach, Meshach, and Abednego! He sent his angel to rescue his servants who trusted in him." And he decreed that anyone who spoke against their God would be destroyed, for "there is no other god who can rescue like this!" (Daniel 3:28–29).

....

Dear God, there is no one else who can rescue like You do!
You make me brave because You are so awesome.

THE GOODNESS OF GOD'S WORD

Every word of God proves true. He is a shield
to all who come to him for protection.
PROVERBS 30:5 NLT

Memorizing scripture is a powerful weapon against fear. God loves to bring verses to your mind exactly when you need them. Sometimes the most calming scriptures, like Psalm 23, repeated in your mind can help you to relax your breathing when you feel panicky. Sometimes singing praises like Psalm 136 are exactly what you need to have joy instead of the fear creeping up on you. Sometimes powerful scripture that recounts the faith of others and the miracles of God, like Hebrews 11, is exactly what you need to grow your faith that God can do any kind of miracle in your situation too. Keep filling your mind with God's Word every chance you get, and see how He uses it to guide you and care for you and protect you.

Dear God, thank You for Your powerful Word.
Bring specific verses to my mind exactly when I
need them to keep my focus fixed on You! Amen.

UNSTOPPABLE LOVE

Since God is for us, who can be against us?
ROMANS 8:31 NLV

Though we might be afraid of certain people some-times, if we stop to remember who it is living in us and working through us—the Holy Spirit of the one and only Creator God Himself—then truly there is no one powerful enough to be against us. There is no one greater than our almighty God who loves us so much He sent His Son to die to save us. Romans 8:38–39 (NLV) goes on to reassure us: "Nothing can keep us from the love of God. Death cannot! Life cannot! Angels cannot! Leaders cannot! Any other power cannot! Hard things now or in the future cannot! The world above or the world below cannot! Any other living thing cannot keep us away from the love of God which is ours through Christ Jesus our Lord."

Dear God, there is no one like You, and I'm grateful to be Your child. Absolutely nothing can keep Your great love away from me, and that fills me with confidence and courage. Thank You! Amen.

MORE ABOUT
ENCOURAGING WORDS

*We should keep on encouraging each other
to be thoughtful and to do helpful things.*
HEBREWS 10:24 CEV

As a writer, I am encouraged when the editor edits my work and adds nice comments about what he or she liked. The editor's words help me not to feel discouraged about the ways I need to improve my writing. One of my favorite movie characters, Mary Poppins, sings, "A Spoonful of Sugar"—the idea behind the lyrics of the song is that something sweet helps us deal with something not so sweet. We can look for ways to encourage someone even when we have to confront them about something hard. And we can appreciate when someone is encouraging us while also confronting or helping to correct our mistakes.

*Dear God, please give me wisdom to give encouragement
generously even when I have to say something hard
for another person to hear, and please help me to
accept correction well when I need to. Amen.*

HEALTHY FEAR

Fear of the LORD is the foundation of true wisdom.
All who obey his commandments will grow in wisdom.
PSALM 111:10 NLT

♡♡

Fear is not always bad. Fear can be good if it motivates us to stay safe. One time on a trip to Chicago for a conference, some friends and I got lost walking around, and it was getting darker and later at night. It was good that we began to be afraid. We had just accidentally taken some wrong turns, and we suddenly realized we had entered a part of town that did not feel safe at all. We didn't know how to find the way back to our hotel. We needed to pray and think hard and fast immediately to get in a safer spot. Thankfully God guided us quickly back to a safer part of town. If we had not listened to fear and just acted silly, we might have gotten ourselves into some really bad situations. Think of a time when you have had a similar experience, and thank God for keeping you safe.

. . . .

Dear God, please give me wisdom about having
healthy fear. Use it when You need to in my life to
keep me protected from harm and to stay on the
good paths You have laid out for me. Amen.

MORE HEALTHY FEAR

Fear of the LORD is the foundation of true knowledge,
but fools despise wisdom and discipline.
PROVERBS 1:7 NLT

♡♡

We should have a healthy fear of a variety of things—fire, for example. One of my very favorite things is sitting around a backyard fire and cooking hot dogs and s'mores. Do you like that too? But we need to respect that any fire can get out of control easily, and take extra care to make sure it stays contained. Medications are another. They are so good when used to help fight illness and relieve pain, but they must be respected for the fact that they can be very dangerous if they are taken too often or in too big of doses. Can you think of other things to have good healthy fear or respect for?

....

Dear God, please guard me and give me good
sense about things that can be dangerous
if I'm not careful with them. Amen.

BRAVE AROUND THE WORLD

Jesus said to them, "You don't need to know the time of those events that only the Father controls. But the Holy Spirit will come upon you and give you power. Then you will tell everyone about me in Jerusalem, in all Judea, in Samaria, and everywhere in the world."
ACTS 1:7–8 CEV

I am very impressed by the courage of friends I know who live in areas of the world where it's not safe for them to be publicly known as Christians. They share their faith with others and hope to lead people to salvation in Jesus, but they do it very carefully because the countries they are in do not give people religious freedom. Remember to pray regularly for those around the world, whether you know any personally or not, who love Jesus and want to share Him with others in countries where it's very dangerous to do so. That is an extra-special kind of courage!

Dear God, please bless and protect missionaries who leave comforts of home countries to go where You send them and share Your truth and love. Amen.

BRAVE ENOUGH TO KEEP PRAYING, PART 1

Three times a day he got down on his knees and prayed, giving thanks to his God, just as he had done before.
DANIEL 6:10 NIV

Daniel was one of the most respected leaders in the land of Babylon. All was well for Daniel until some jealous leaders went to King Darius and convinced him to make a law that would throw anyone in the lions' den who prayed to anyone besides the king. But Daniel loved the one true God and continued to pray to Him three times a day in front of his open window. The jealous leaders quickly went to the king to report what Daniel was doing. So Daniel was thrown into the den of lions.

Dear God, please help me to have courage never to stop believing in You and praying to You, even if I am in danger for doing so. You are bigger and stronger than anything any person can do to me. Amen.

BRAVE ENOUGH TO KEEP PRAYING, PART 2

The king said to Daniel, "May your God, whom you serve continually, rescue you!" A stone was brought and placed over the mouth of the den, and the king sealed it with his own signet ring and with the rings of his nobles, so that Daniel's situation might not be changed. Then the king returned to his palace and spent the night without eating and without any entertainment being brought to him. And he could not sleep.
DANIEL 6:16–18 NIV

The next morning after David was thrown into the lions' den, the king hurried to the den and called out, "Daniel, servant of the living God, has your God been able to save you from the lions?"

And Daniel answered! "My God sent his angel and shut the mouths of the lions. He knows I am not guilty. I have done nothing wrong before you either, O king."

The king ordered Daniel out of the lions' den. Daniel didn't even have a scratch on his body!

....

Dear God, like You protected Daniel when he stayed faithful to You, I know You will protect me too. Remind me of Daniel when I need to be brave. Amen.

WHEN FEAR MEANS RESPECT, PART 1

*Let the whole world fear the L*ORD*,*
and let everyone stand in awe of him.
PSALM 33:8 NLT

♡♡

You may read this scripture and think, *What? I thought this was a book about courage, and this verse is telling me I should fear God?* Yes, because one meaning of the word *fear* is "to revere or respect or be in awe." This verse goes on to say that everyone should stand in awe of Him! If you've ever been to Niagara Falls or the Grand Canyon, you should know what it's like to respect and be in awe of something that is mind-blowingly cool. You respect the fact that there is incredible danger about great waterfalls and gigantic canyons if you should happen to fall into them, and you also think of how awesome they are and how amazing it is that they exist! We should think of God with total respect and wonder, knowing that He is capable of danger because He holds all power, but being grateful that He loves us dearly as His children.

Dear God, I fear You in the best sense of the word.
I love and respect You with all my heart. Please keep
growing me in love and respect for You! Amen.

WHEN FEAR MEANS RESPECT, PART 2

*Fear the Lord, you his godly people, for those
who fear him will have all they need.*
Psalm 34:9 NLT

♡♡

Look at some more of the scriptures that talk about fearing God the right way, because love and respect for Him and following His ways are what keep you close to Him. And when you are close to Him, you have nothing to fear, for He is always taking the best care of you!

"The Lord is a friend to those who fear him." (Psalm 25:14 NLT)

"Whoever fears the Lord has a secure fortress, and for their children it will be a refuge. The fear of the Lord is a fountain of life, turning a person from the snares of death." (Proverbs 14:26–27 NIV)

"Fear of the Lord leads to life, bringing security and protection from harm." (Proverbs 19:23 NLT)

"Fear God and obey his commands, for this is everyone's duty." (Ecclesiastes 12:13 NLT)

....

*Dear God, thank You for the many reminders in
Your Word to respect and follow You. I'm grateful
for the good way You take care of me! Amen.*

IN FRONT OF THE CLASS

I will always trust in God's unfailing love. I will praise
you forever, O God, for what you have done.
PSALM 52:8–9 NLT

Giving a speech or presentation at school can be super scary sometimes. You might wonder if you'll forget everything you meant to say or if you'll accidentally do something embarrassing and make your classmates laugh at you. My voice used to shake like I was about to cry every single time I had to speak in front of the class. And that made me feel so silly. I think in those times, the best way to have courage is to think about how no matter how the speech or presentation goes, nothing changes God's love for you and nothing changes the love that your family and friends have for you. So stand up with confidence and courage in all the love God gives you, because that's far more important than any kind of public speaking.

Dear God, please help me not to stress over a speech
or presentation, for I know at the beginning of it,
during it, and when it's over I'm completely
loved by You! Thank You! Amen.

NO FEAR OF FALLING

*"I will look to the Lord for help. I will wait for God to save
me. My God will hear me. Enemy, don't laugh at me.
I have fallen, but I will get up again. I sit in the shadow
of trouble now. But the Lord will be a light for me."*
MICAH 7:7–8 ICB

Have you ever had a dream where you're free-
falling and don't know when you'll ever stop? It's such
a scary feeling! I've woken up from those dreams
with a jolt before, very glad to realize I was actually
safe and sound. We might have some fears of actually falling if, for instance, we're trying to roller-skate
and we're not all that great, and we might have some
figurative fears of falling, as in the sense of failing or
losing. Either way, we can trust that God will help us
get back up. Our courage comes from knowing that
no matter if we succeed or fail, God takes care of us!

*Dear God, thank You for always lifting
me back up after any kind of fall. Amen.*

WILLING TO LET GO

Don't store up treasures on earth! Moths and rust can destroy them, and thieves can break in and steal them. Instead, store up your treasures in heaven, where moths and rust cannot destroy them, and thieves cannot break in and steal them. Your heart will always be where your treasure is.
MATTHEW 6:19–21 CEV

♡♡

We all have favorite items, maybe toys or stuffed animals or little collections we've kept. But as you grow and get older, you can't hang on to things forever. Even though it might be sad to go through old things and get rid of them, you need to develop courage to do it. Sharing things you don't have much use for or play with anymore can be a blessing to others who might be in need. And it creates space for new things and interests you might have as you grow older. So be brave enough to let go and be generous with others.

....

Dear God, help me not to hang on too tightly to things that are just things. Help me to be generous and share, and also to keep my stuff organized and not overwhelming. Amen.

LESSON LEARNED, PART 1

Jonah was in the belly of the
fish three days and three nights.
JONAH 1:17 NIV

♡♡

Jonah's story is an example of what can happen when God asks us to be courageous for a specific task and we don't listen. Jonah didn't want to go to Nineveh and preach there like God asked him to do, so he made his own plan and sailed in the opposite direction. But God sent such a strong storm that the boat Jonah was sailing on nearly broke apart—until the sailors threw Jonah into the sea. Then a large fish swallowed Jonah and kept him in its belly for three days! While he sat in that fish's belly, Jonah prayed and worshipped God. And then God told the fish to spit Jonah out onto dry land.

....

Dear God, please remind me of Jonah when I feel like
doing my own thing instead of obeying You. Help me
to be brave to obey and remember that there can
be bad consequences if I don't. Amen.

LESSON LEARNED,
PART 2

Then the word of the Lord came to Jonah a second
time: "Go to the great city of Nineveh and proclaim to
it the message I give you." Jonah obeyed the word
of the Lord and went to Nineveh.
JONAH 3:1–3 NIV

After the whale spit out Jonah, once again God told Jonah to get up and go to Nineveh to preach to the people there. Jonah had learned his lesson not to disobey God. He did not run away this time. He went to Nineveh and bravely preached as God directed. And because the people listened and turned away from their sin, God saved their city from destruction.

Dear God, help me to learn the lesson from Jonah
that I need to listen the first time when You ask me to
do something. I want to obey You bravely, and I want
to see You do amazing things through me when I do.
Thank You for saving the people of Nineveh. Amen.

IN THE DARK VALLEYS

Even when I walk through the darkest valley,
I will not be afraid, for you are close beside me.
PSALM 23:4 NLT

You've probably walked through some dark valleys in your life, times when maybe you felt very hurt by a friend or lost a loved one. Or maybe you're disappointed or in a lot of worry and fear. God never promises that we won't experience those hard things, but He does promise He is close beside us as we go through them. I know firsthand that it's during the worst and most painful moments that God has felt the very closest. When you feel you're in a dark valley, ask God to show you how close He is and how much He cares. He will answer you in many ways and through many people and sources.

Dear God, You are my source of love and light and
courage during any dark times. Thank You! Amen.

KEEP ON AND ON AND ON

Even when I am afraid, I keep on trusting you.
I praise your promises! I trust you and am
not afraid. No one can harm me.
PSALM 56:3–4 CEV

♡♡

My daughters, Jodi and Lilly, love to dance, but if they just dance for a while and then stop and never practice again, they're not dancers anymore. They have to *keep on* dancing and stretching and dancing some more. And if we want to be courageous girls, we have to *keep on* trusting God even when we're afraid. We can't just say we trusted God once, and that's it. We should want the constant action of choosing trust again and again each day, knowing we face new challenges and realizing how we must focus on and believe in God's perfect promises to guide us through them and protect us in the midst of them.

Dear God, again today I choose to keep on trusting You!
I want this to be my prayer every day! Amen.

COURAGE FOR BIG TESTS

*Trust in the LORD with all your heart and lean not on
your own understanding; in all your ways submit
to him, and he will make your paths straight.*
PROVERBS 3:5–6 NIV

Do you take big tests for school that scare you sometimes? A lot of worry may surround them, as you wonder if you will do well or if you'll forget what you've
studied and learned. And sometimes teachers hype
them up so big that it's hard not to lose sleep at night
over them. It's good to care about your tests, but
it's not good to care so much that you make yourself
sick with fear or anxiety about them. If you regularly
strive to do your best with schoolwork and you study
well and do your best, then just relax about tests and
trust God with the results!

*Dear God, please calm my fears and nervousness when a
big test is looming. Please help me think clearly and do
my best and trust that You're always helping me. Amen.*

REMEMBER THE COWARDLY LION

*My health may fail, and my spirit may
grow weak, but God remains the strength
of my heart; he is mine forever.*
PSALM 73:26 NLT

You probably know the story of the Cowardly Lion in the *Wizard of Oz.* He tries to act tough at first but soon shows the truth when Dorothy stands up to him for picking on her friends and especially her tiny dog, Toto. The lion admits he's afraid of pretty much everything. Soon he joins the quest to find the wizard and decides he'll ask the wizard to give him courage. It's a fun fiction story to think of when you pray and ask God for courage. But thankfully our almighty God is not fiction at all. He is real and true and can always give you courage for any scary situation. Just ask Him!

*Dear God, I know You are real and true.
I need You to give me real and true courage.
Will You, please? Thank You! Amen.*

GOD TAKES GOOD CARE OF YOU

The Lord is right and good in all His ways, and kind in all His works. The Lord is near to all who call on Him, to all who call on Him in truth. He will fill the desire of those who fear Him. He will also hear their cry and will save them. The Lord takes care of all who love Him.
PSALM 145:17–20 NLV

Who is the most trustworthy person you know? And I hope you are a very trustworthy person too! But no matter how trustworthy and honest anyone on this planet is, they are never perfect in every single thing they do. Each person makes mistakes or lets us down. But as Psalm 145:17 tells us, God is right and good and kind in all His works. He never makes mistakes, and He hears and saves all of us who love and respect Him. Thank Him for all the good and trustworthy people in your life, but praise Him most of all for being the One who *never* lets you down!

Dear God, I feel brave when I remember how You are perfect in all of Your ways and You take perfect care of me. Amen.

LIFE AND POWER THAT COMES FROM GOD

I fall to my knees and pray to the Father, the Creator of everything in heaven and on earth. I pray that from his glorious, unlimited resources he will empower you with inner strength through his Spirit. Then Christ will make his home in your hearts as you trust in him. Your roots will grow down into God's love and keep you strong. And may you have the power to understand, as all God's people should, how wide, how long, how high, and how deep his love is. May you experience the love of Christ, though it is too great to understand fully. Then you will be made complete with all the fullness of life and power that comes from God.
EPHESIANS 3:14–19 NLT

Paul wrote this powerful prayer in the book of Ephesians, which is for you today too. God has unlimited power to strengthen you. Jesus lives in you as you trust in Him, growing stronger and stronger. And God's love for you is too big to be measured. If all this awesome truth doesn't give you great confidence and courage, I'm not sure what will!

Dear God, thank You for the power of Your Word to encourage me in exactly the right ways to make me confident and brave! Amen.

STANDING FIRM

Therefore, my dear brothers and sisters,
stand firm. Let nothing move you. Always
give yourselves fully to the work of the Lord.
1 CORINTHIANS 15:58 NIV

♡ ♡

Do you have a carnival or festival you like to go to in your town? My very favorite carnival ride was always the swings when I was your age. I loved the breezy feeling while flying around and around. Now, though, any kind of around-and-around ride makes me far too dizzy. I get off feeling like the whole world is moving under my feet—I definitely don't feel like I can stand firm. In this scripture, Paul writes to Christians to stand firm and let nothing move us as we give ourselves completely to God to do the good things He has planned for us. We don't want to be dizzy with fears or distractions that could make us fall. We want courage and strength and consistency as we follow and serve Jesus.

Dear God, help me to stand strong and firm
in my faith in You and in my willingness to
do whatever work You ask of me. Amen.

BRAVE LIKE THE DISCIPLES

*As Jesus was walking beside the Sea of Galilee,
he saw two brothers, Simon called Peter and his brother
Andrew. They were casting a net into the lake, for they
were fishermen. "Come, follow me," Jesus said, "and I will
send you out to fish for people." At once they left their
nets and followed him. Going on from there, he saw two
other brothers, James son of Zebedee and his brother
John. They were in a boat with their father Zebedee,
preparing their nets. Jesus called them, and immediately
they left the boat and their father and followed him.*
MATTHEW 4:18–22 NIV

When Jesus started His ministry of teaching and healing, He wanted close friends to come alongside Him, travel with Him, learn from Him, and help people believe in Him. These close friends were called His disciples. Think of what courage it must have taken for them to leave the jobs they had known as fishermen to suddenly begin a whole new life with Jesus!

*Dear Jesus, help me to be brave like the disciples.
If You call to me, I want to be ready to drop
everything else and do anything You ask! Amen.*

BRAVER WITH GOOD FRIENDS

A friend loves at all times.
A brother is born to share troubles.
PROVERBS 17:17 NLV

Just as Jesus wanted close friends, you need good close friends in your life too. And it's important to choose wisely. You want friends who feel as close as family and who encourage you and help you be stronger and braver in the good plans God has for you. You don't want friends who pull you away from following God or who distract you with meaningless things. You want real friends who help you through troubles and who help make you sharp! Proverbs 27:17 (CEV) says, "Just as iron sharpens iron, friends sharpen the minds of each other."

Dear God, please bring the right friends into my life who encourage me always to follow You and who help make me brave and sharp! Amen.

STORM STOPPER

*A bad wind storm came up. The waves were coming
over the side of the boat. It was filling up with water.
Jesus was in the back part of the boat sleeping on a
pillow. They woke Him up, crying out, "Teacher, do You
not care that we are about to die?" He got up and
spoke sharp words to the wind. He said to the sea,
"Be quiet! Be still." At once the wind stopped blowing.*
MARK 4:37–39 NLV

♡♡

I love boat rides, but I have never been on a boat
during a major storm. I have felt a cruise ship rock-
ing side to side in big waves, but that was no big deal.
I've heard of far worse and thankfully have not experienced it. Have you ever been on a super scary boat
ride? I can't imagine how terrified Jesus' disciples
must have been during the storm described in Mark
4. Yet it took only a moment for Jesus to speak and
make everything okay.

*Dear Jesus, help me to remember this story, and build my
faith because of it. You are capable of simply speaking
the words and stopping anything scary. I believe You
are always able to do that in my life too! Amen.*

BRAVE LOVE,
PART 1

You have heard people say, "Love your neighbors and hate your enemies." But I tell you to love your enemies and pray for anyone who mistreats you. Then you will be acting like your Father in heaven.
MATTHEW 5:43–45 CEV

A hard scripture to read is this one about loving your enemies. That sure takes a lot of courage and determination. If a classmate is being mean to you at school, the last thing you feel like doing is loving them. But that's the kind of brave thing God asks of us who love Him, and He gives us the power to do it. He doesn't mean you have to be bullied and abused. You need to be wise about the way you show love to enemies. But, absolutely, you can pray for them and ask God to help you love them like He does.

Dear God, even when it's incredibly hard, please give me the courage and wisdom to love my enemies. Show me what to do. Thank You! Amen.

BRAVE LOVE,
PART 2

*Ask God to bless everyone who mistreats you. Ask him
to bless them and not to curse them. When others
are happy, be happy with them, and when they
are sad, be sad. Be friendly with everyone.*
ROMANS 12:14–16 CEV

When others are being mean, you can also choose to
do your best to act in kindness and do the right thing
even though they are not. You can stand up to them
without being mean back at them. Ask God to show
you how to love and interact with enemies and stay
patient as He does a big and mighty work through
you! Who knows how He might help you change a
bully's heart?

. . . .

*Dear God, help me always to be kind but to
remember that I can stick up for myself and others
too. I want to show Your love in the right ways.
Please help me to be smart about this. Amen.*

BUILT UP FOR BRAVERY, PART 1

*Anyone who hears and obeys these teachings
of mine is like a wise person who built a house
on solid rock. Rain poured down, rivers flooded,
and winds beat against that house. But it did
not fall, because it was built on solid rock.*
MATTHEW 7:24–25 CEV

♡♡

I've seen some really great sandcastles at the beach!
Some people are amazing artists with sand. Maybe
you are too! But a sandcastle never lasts for too long
in the waves and weather. Jesus warned about building our spiritual houses on sand. He said that anything
built on a strong foundation like rock is able to stand
firm through all kinds of weather. If you build your life
strong on the rock of Jesus and His Word, you will
stand firm and brave through all kinds of situations.

*Dear Jesus, please build me up on Your Word to
be strong and brave in it as long as I live. Amen.*

BUILT UP FOR BRAVERY, PART 2

Anyone who hears my teachings and doesn't obey them is like a foolish person who built a house on sand. The rain poured down, the rivers flooded, and the winds blew and beat against that house. Finally, it fell with a crash.
MATTHEW 7:26–27 CEV

Jesus went on to say how anything built on sand is not strong enough to last. Jesus was comparing people who hear His teaching and listen and obey it to people who only hear it but do nothing with it. Those who obey Jesus are built up strong and brave for whatever life brings their way, while those who ignore Jesus are easily washed away.

Dear Jesus, I don't want to ignore You and easily wash away in my faith in You! Please build me up with strength and courage, depending on You as my rock in every kind of weather! Amen.

EVEN IN THE LITTLE THINGS

"There's a young boy here with five barley loaves and two fish. But what good is that with this huge crowd?" "Tell everyone to sit down," Jesus said. So they all sat down on the grassy slopes. (The men alone numbered about 5,000.) Then Jesus took the loaves, gave thanks to God, and distributed them to the people. Afterward he did the same with the fish. And they all ate as much as they wanted.
JOHN 6:9–11 NLT

♡♡

Bravery in big things might be what makes most of the news headlines. But bravery in small things is important too. Think about what a great thing Jesus did with a small act of bravery from a young boy who gave up his lunch. It might not seem like too big of a deal, but the boy probably was a little worried he might not get to eat that day! And then Jesus did an amazing miracle, taking that little lunch and feeding a huge crowd of people with many baskets left over. Think about how many of those people must have believed in Jesus that day after seeing such a stunning miracle. Be faithful and brave in even the smallest thing God calls you to do. Who knows how He will use it?

Dear God, I want to be brave even in the little things You ask of me. Show me how You will use everything I offer You. Amen.

COURAGE TO VISIT

*In my old age, don't set me aside. Don't
abandon me when my strength is failing.*
PSALM 71:9 NLT

You might think that visiting a nursing home can be intimidating or scary. Maybe you have a grandparent or loved one who lives in one and you enjoy visiting them, but you're not sure how to interact with other residents who might have health problems or disabilities. Don't let those worries and fears stop you. People in nursing homes need encouragement! I've spent a lot of time visiting nursing homes, and it's so rewarding to brighten the residents' days with a kind word, a smile, or a chat. Ask God to help you never be afraid to reach out and encourage those who are elderly and those who are struggling with their health.

*Dear God, please help me not to be scared to visit with
elderly people who need my encouragement. Amen.*

WALKING ON WATER, PART 1

Later that night, he was there alone, and the boat was already a considerable distance from land, buffeted by the waves because the wind was against it. Shortly before dawn Jesus went out to them, walking on the lake.
MATTHEW 14:23–25 NIV

Once when Jesus went off to pray alone, the disciples were in a boat traveling on ahead of Him. Then, in the middle of the night, He walked out on the lake to catch up with them. The Bible says the disciples were terrified. "It's a ghost," they said, and cried out in fear. But Jesus immediately said to them, "Take courage! It is I. Don't be afraid."

Somehow it's comforting to read that Jesus' disciples spent so much time learning from Him and yet sometimes still struggled with fear. It's reassuring that Jesus knows and understands that even though we grow close to Him, we will sometimes struggle with fear too. When we do, He will always remind us that He is near.

....

Dear Jesus, You are truly able to do any kind of miracle, even walking on water! I feel so brave knowing You are with me and are able to help me with anything I need! Amen.

WALKING ON WATER, PART 2

"Lord, if it's you," Peter replied, "tell me to come to you on the water." "Come," he said. Then Peter got down out of the boat, walked on the water and came toward Jesus. But when he saw the wind, he was afraid and, beginning to sink, cried out, "Lord, save me!" Immediately Jesus reached out his hand and caught him. "You of little faith," he said, "why did you doubt?"
MATTHEW 14:28–31 NIV

As soon as the disciple Peter heard it was Jesus out on the lake, he wanted to walk on water too! And he trusted, with great courage, in Jesus' ability to make it happen. So he started out just fine walking on the waves toward Jesus! But then something changed. He noticed the weather and began to sink. What had happened? Peter took his focus off of Jesus and put it on fear of the wind and waves instead. The same thing will happen to us if we let it. We must keep our focus on Jesus through any kind of scary situation. If we do, He'll keep us brave and steady, but if we don't, we will begin to sink.

Dear Jesus, I want to stay focused on You and Your power to do anything! Please help me! Amen.

COURAGE NOT TO QUIT

*Christ gives me the strength
to face anything.*
PHILIPPIANS 4:13 CEV

Have you ever badly wanted to quit something? Maybe you wished you could drop out of a class at school because it felt way too hard. Or maybe you tried a new sport but didn't want to finish the season. I've been there for sure. I've had classes and jobs that have stressed me out so much I didn't think I would survive. But I look back and see how God was giving me courage and strength to take things one day at a time. And now I see how He used that time to grow me into a better person when I endured instead of quitting. In any hard situation, if you call on God to help, then trust in and wait on Him, He will either help you walk through it day by day until it's over or help you find a wise way out immediately.

Dear God, please help me when I want to quit in a hard situation. Give me courage and wisdom. Amen.

COURAGE TO GIVE IT ALL

A poor widow came and dropped in two small coins.
MARK 12:42 NLT

♡♡

One day Jesus watched as many rich people gave large offerings to God at the temple. This wasn't hard for them to do because they were so rich that they had plenty of money to share. But then Jesus watched one woman, who was terribly poor and had no husband, drop in two very small copper coins. Added together, the two coins weren't even worth one whole cent.

Jesus saw this, and He called out to His disciples, "This is the truth—this poor widow has given more money than all the others."

How could this be? The widow had only given two small coins that didn't even amount to a penny! And the rich people had given a whole bunch of money—a lot more than the poor widow.

But Jesus said, "The rich people put in money they didn't even need because they have so much extra. But the poor widow has nothing extra. She needed every bit of her money to live on, but still she gave it all to God."

. . . .

Dear God, help me to have great courage in You just like the widow in Jesus' story. She trusted You to provide for her no matter what, even if she gave until she had nothing left, and I want to give to You in that same kind of way. Amen.

WATCHING A SQUIRREL

For we are God's masterpiece. He has created
us anew in Christ Jesus, so we can do the
good things he planned for us long ago.
EPHESIANS 2:10 NLT

This past winter I smiled with delight and amazement when I noticed a squirrel climbing higher and higher and higher in the bare branches of one of our backyard willow trees. He had no fear of the great height he was at. What a brave little squirrel! But to him it was nothing because he was just doing what squirrels do. I would never be brave enough to climb that high in a tree. Is that a problem I need more courage for? No, because there's no purpose for it in my life. I only need to be brave to be prepared for the things God asks of me, has created me for, and has planned for me to do—and so do you!

Dear God, help me to be inspired by bravery I see around me—even from squirrels! But also help me to remember that I only need to be brave for the things You ask me to do. You give certain abilities and tasks to some people and different ones to others. Amen.

COURAGE TO COME HOME AGAIN, PART 1

*"This younger son packed all his belongings
and moved to a distant land, and there
he wasted all his money in wild living."*
LUKE 15:13 NLT

One of Jesus' parables was about a father who divided all that he owned between his two sons. The younger son took all of his inheritance and went to another country far away. He spent everything on living a wild and foolish life. After all of his money was gone, he was hungry, but because of a famine, there was no food in the land. The only job he could find was feeding pigs. Then he began to think about what he had done and was ashamed of himself. He said to himself, *I should go home to my father. I will say to him, "Father, I have sinned against heaven and against you. I am not good enough to be called your son. But could I work for you?"* So the son got up and went to his father.

....

Dear Father, please help me to have courage to realize when I've done wrong and be willing to return to make things right. Thank You that You love me no matter what, and thank You for the people in my life who love me no matter what. Amen.

COURAGE TO COME HOME AGAIN, PART 2

"We had to celebrate this happy day."
Luke 15:32 NLT

♡♡

While the younger son was still a long way off, his father saw him and felt full of love and kindness toward him. He ran to his son and threw his arms around him and kissed him. The son said, "Father, I have sinned against heaven and against you. I am not good enough to be called your son."

But the father said to his workmen, "Hurry! Get the best coat and put it on him. Put a ring on his hand and shoes on his feet. Bring the fat calf and kill it so we can eat it. Let's be glad, because my son was lost and now he is found. Let's eat and have a good time."

....

Dear God, the father in this parable had to have great courage too—the kind of courage that helps us forgive in big ways. He had to forgive his son and love him fully and trust that he wouldn't run off again. I want to have that kind of courage and grace for others too. Amen.

COURAGE FOR FACING
MEAN GIRLS

*"Be strong and courageous. Do not fear
or be in dread of them, for it is the
Lord your God who goes with you."*
DEUTERONOMY 31:6 ESV

Have you ever had to deal with mean girls? Girls who are always looking for a fight and causing trouble and creating drama? Girls like that can make school miserable, and you need a lot of courage to keep on going. Be sure to pray hard for wisdom on how to handle situations with mean girls. Maybe you'll have to work in group projects together, or maybe you'll need to stick up for a friend the mean girls are picking on. Or maybe you'll be the one being picked on. Whatever the case, God will give you wisdom and help when you ask. Pray for the hearts of the mean girls too. Pray for them to be changed by the love of God and for them to see God's love through you!

*Dear God, help me to be brave to face mean girls,
and give me wisdom to interact with them. Please
turn their hearts toward You and Your love. Amen.*

A-OKAY

*We know that God is always at work for
the good of everyone who loves him.*
ROMANS 8:28 CEV

When you're going through a hard time, it's easy to feel discouraged. That's the opposite of encouraged, so you might feel like you have zero courage to do anything! That's when remembering Romans 8:28 is so good. This scripture promises that God is always working things out for good for people who love Him. If you love Him, are trusting in Jesus as your Savior, and are living for Him, God is working in every kind of situation—even the hardest and weirdest ones—and will make them okay in the end. I don't know about you, but I need to be reminded of this truth all the time.

*Dear God, when I feel discouraged, remind me
that You are always working for my good.
I am so grateful for that! Amen.*

BRAVER WITH MUSIC

Worship the LORD with gladness. Come before him, singing with joy. Acknowledge that the LORD is God! He made us, and we are his.
PSALM 100:2–3 NLT

♡♡

One of our very favorite things to watch at our house is *The Sound of Music*. As it was on in our living room the other day, I stopped to think about how much courage Maria had to have to take on a whole new life and new role of governess, or nanny, to seven children. I love how she sings her way into more confidence in the movie. We can sing when we need extra confidence or courage too. Praise songs to God remind us of His power and goodness. He is the very best source of confidence and courage for any new thing we're about to do or any hard situation we are in.

Dear God, please help me to have joy and be able to sing even when I'm feeling scared or nervous. I know music can help calm me down, especially with songs of praise to You! Amen.

PRINCESS UNDER PROTECTION

For those who are led by the Spirit of God are the children of God. The Spirit you received does not make you slaves, so that you live in fear again; rather, the Spirit you received brought about your adoption to sonship And by him we cry, "Abba, Father."
ROMANS 8:14–15 NIV

When you trust Christ as Savior and receive the Holy Spirit, you become a child of God! He is King of all kings and Lord of all lords, and you are His child. That truly means you are royalty. Think of what it means to be a princess under the protection of the King! That's you! Your heavenly King Father is not just some distant kind of dad but is one you can think of as running to for a big bear hug! He loves and cares for you very much and never wants you to live in fear about anything.

Dear heavenly Daddy, thank You for loving me so much and keeping me under Your royal protection. Amen.

THE BRAVE GOOD SAMARITAN, PART 1

Jesus replied with a story: "A Jewish man was traveling from Jerusalem down to Jericho, and he was attacked by bandits."
LUKE 10:30 NLT

♡♡

Do you know the story that Jesus told about the good Samaritan? Nasty robbers stole everything from a Jewish man, even his clothes. Then they beat him and left him to die on the side of the road.

Soon a religious leader called a priest came by on the same road. He saw the poor man, but he walked right past on the other side of the road.

Next, a man from the family of Levi passed by. But the Levite did not help either!

Finally, a man called a Samaritan—who normally would have had *nothing* to do with a Jewish man because there was great hatred among Jews and Samaritans—saw the poor Jewish man lying alongside the road. The Samaritan felt sorry for the Jewish man and helped him.

. . . .

Dear God, it took a lot of courage for the Samaritan to stop and help the Jewish man. Please help me to be brave to set aside differences and be willing to help others too. Amen.

THE BRAVE GOOD SAMARITAN, PART 2

"The Samaritan soothed his wounds with olive oil and wine and bandaged them. Then he put the man on his own donkey and took him to an inn, where he took care of him. The next day he handed the innkeeper two silver coins, telling him, 'Take care of this man. If his bill runs higher than this, I'll pay you the next time I'm here.'"
LUKE 10:34–35 NLT

With compassion, the Samaritan went to the man and cared for his wounds and bandaged them. Then the Samaritan helped the injured man onto a donkey, took him to an inn, and paid for him to have a safe place to rest and get well.

When Jesus was done sharing this story, He asked the religious expert, "Which of the three men was a neighbor to the man who was attacked by the robbers?"

And the religious leader said, "The one who helped."

And Jesus said, "That's right. Now go and do the same kind of thing."

Dear Jesus, please give me the courage I need to obey You in this kind of love for others. Amen.

NEVER ABANDONED
OR DESTROYED

*We are pressed on every side by troubles, but we are not
crushed. We are perplexed, but not driven to despair.
We are hunted down, but never abandoned by God.
We get knocked down, but we are not destroyed.*
2 CORINTHIANS 4:8–9 NLT

We've all had days when every single thing seems to be
going wrong. Maybe we even have weeks or months
like that, times when we feel so discouraged we wonder when God is *ever* going to step in to help rescue
us or at least protect us from any more trouble. This
scripture promises that no matter how discouraged
we feel, God will never let us get to a point where we
cannot handle our discouragement. Sometimes He
will wait to the last moment, but He will always provide a way out. He lets us experience hard things at
times to teach us new lessons and show us how brave
and strong we can be in all kinds of situations when
we depend on Him.

*Dear God, please help me to keep hanging in there
when I feel discouraged. I know You never abandon me,
and You have good plans for me. Amen.*

A HORSE NAMED SAMMY, PART 1

When we get together, I want to encourage you in your faith, but I also want to be encouraged by yours.
ROMANS 1:12 NLT

♡♡

When I was little, my family had a horse named Sammy who loved to knock down her fence and escape her pasture. One morning while I waited for the school bus, she got loose and came up to our front porch. A horse at my door was a hilarious sight for all the kids on the bus to see! We finally figured out that Sammy kept leaving the pasture because she was lonely. She was used to having cows in the pasture, but our family had recently sold them. So she was just looking for company! Sometimes we feel lonely too, and that can make us feel scared. It's good to admit when we're lonely and then have courage to reach out to family and friends and share those feelings. Soon you'll be feeling better as you do things together instead of alone.

....

Dear God, please help me when I feel alone. I know You are always with me, but You also want to provide people to give me good company. So much of Your love for me comes through other people, and I am thankful! Amen.

A HORSE NAMED SAMMY, PART 2

I prayed to the LORD, and he answered me.
He freed me from all my fears.
PSALM 34:4 NLT

♡ ♡

Sammy the horse was very skittish at times. One time while I was riding and my dad was leading, he reached down to the grass to pick up a pop can and threw it into the driveway to remember to put in the trash later. Well, that simple action spooked Sammy so much that she startled and whirled around. I flew off of her back and onto my bottom on the ground. Ouch! Thankfully I wasn't hurt badly. I took a break and didn't get back on Sammy that day, but I didn't let the scary incident keep me off horses forever. I did ride again and even once went riding on a gorgeous ranch in Montana, which was so cool! When we have scary experiences, we need to remember that if we let them control us, they might keep us from wonderful experiences in the future.

....

Dear God, thank You for protecting me during scary incidents, and please help me not to be controlled by fear of them. I don't want to miss out on future experiences and blessings because of fear! Amen.

SLICK AND SLIPPERY

*When I felt my feet slipping, you came with your love and
kept me steady. And when I was burdened with worries,
you comforted me and made me feel secure.*
PSALM 94:18–19 CEV

If you live in an area where winter is long and cold,
you probably know the feeling of your feet slipping.
Ice and snow make everything slick, and you have to
be extra careful not to fall. Or if you do fall, you want
to make sure you have a big pile of fluffy snow to
land in! When you read Psalm 94, you can think of
that slippery feeling but then picture God's strong
hand reaching out to steady you and keep you safe.
In any slippery situation, you can have courage remembering that God is always ready to reach out and
help you.

*Dear God, thank You for being the One who
steadies me. I don't need to be scared of
anything with You so near. Amen.*

THE COURAGE OF ZACCHAEUS, PART 1

[Zacchaeus] tried to get a look at Jesus,
but he was too short to see over the crowd.
LUKE 19:3 NLT

♡♡

Zacchaeus was a wealthy man, a chief tax collector who lived in Jesus' time. Men like him were known for being unfair. They cheated and took far too much of other people's money. So most people in Jericho hated and avoided Zacchaeus.

But Zacchaeus was drawn to Jesus and wanted to do whatever it took to see Jesus as He traveled through Jericho. Even though Zacchaeus was not very tall and it would be hard for him to find a good view among the crowds of people, he was determined. He ran ahead of where Jesus would walk, and he climbed a big tree, a sycamore tree! High in the branches, he waited and watched for the One called the Son of God.

Dear Jesus, even if people don't like me or
I have challenges to overcome, help me to
be brave and determined like Zacchaeus
to want to be close to You! Amen.

THE COURAGE OF ZACCHAEUS, PART 2

Zacchaeus quickly climbed down and took Jesus
to his house in great excitement and joy.
LUKE 19:6 NLT

Soon Jesus was traveling by! And when He reached that sycamore tree that Zacchaeus was in, He stopped and spotted Zacchaeus. Then He called him by name and said, "Come down right away. I am going to your house today."

Zacchaeus was totally amazed and very excited! He happily climbed down at once and welcomed Jesus to his home.

As Zacchaeus spent time with Jesus, he was sorry for his sins. He wanted to make all his wrongs right. He wanted to help the poor. He wanted to give back to people all the money he had cheated them out of, plus four times more!

Dear God, thank You for the example of Zacchaeus
who was brave to watch for You and welcome You
and brave to admit his mistakes and want to do
everything to make them right. Amen.

AFRAID OF NO ONE

*Don't be afraid of anyone! Everything that is hidden
will be found out, and every secret will be known.*
MATTHEW 10:26 CEV

If you've ever dealt with bullies at school, they usually
have to try to be sneaky to be mean. This scripture
reminds you not to be afraid of them, because they
will be found out—if not right away, then eventually.
Teachers and school staff are usually on the lookout
for bullies, so they will get in trouble. And ultimately
God sees and cares and will bring consequences and
justice. Keep praying to Him to do that and for wisdom on how to stand up to bullies, and for protection
and courage too!

. . . .

*Dear God, remind me all the time that I don't need to be
afraid of anyone. You see and know everything and will
make everything right in Your perfect timing. Amen.*

FIGHTING THE ENEMY

*The devil is working against you. He is walking
around like a hungry lion with his mouth open.
He is looking for someone to eat. Stand against
him and be strong in your faith.*
1 PETER 5:8–9 NLV

To really have courage doesn't mean you pretend there's nothing to be afraid of. This scripture
shares the hard truth that we Christians definitely
have an enemy—the devil—who is like a lion wanting
to destroy us. We need to know about him and have
courage to fight him. And how do we fight him? By
staying close to God. Read His Word, pray constantly,
be involved in a Bible-teaching church that helps you
grow closer to God. Pursue friendship with people
who encourage and support you in your faith, and be
very careful to keep distance from people who lead
you in bad ways. The devil wants to destroy us by
getting us alone or with bad influences and tempting
us into disobeying God. But we can stand up to him
and fight with the power God gives us!

*Dear God, please help me to be watchful of the devil and
be bravely ready to fight him in Your power. Amen.*

THE ULTIMATE WINNERS

A thief comes only to rob, kill, and destroy.
I came so that everyone would have life,
and have it in its fullest.
JOHN 10:10 CEV

♡♡

We can take great courage in the fact that no matter what the devil tries to do to us, we will always win against him in the end. He might hurt us or make us stumble away from God at times, but he will never totally defeat us when we trust in Jesus as our Savior. This scripture tells us that the devil wants to steal and destroy every good thing, but Jesus came to give us life to the fullest. When Jesus died but rose again, He showed that absolutely nothing the devil does can ever defeat the powerful love of God and His desire to give us everlasting life with Him!

Dear God, thank You so much that Jesus rose to life again after death! He is proof of Your gift of eternal life for me. Nothing can ever take away that most valuable gift, and that makes me feel so brave! Amen.

BRAVELY BELIEVING, PART 1

*A man who worked with the king had a son who
was sick in the city of Capernaum. This man went
to Jesus. . . . The man asked Jesus if He would go
to Capernaum and heal his son who was dying.*
JOHN 4:46–47 NLV

♡♡

Do you know the story of the nobleman who believed
Jesus? He had government authority over Jesus, but
he respected Jesus. The nobleman came to Jesus and
said, "Sir, I'm begging You to heal my son. Please come
to him before he dies!" And Jesus said, "You may go.
Your son will live."

But that's not exactly what the nobleman wanted
to hear! He thought surely Jesus needed to actually
be with his son to heal him. And with his authority,
the nobleman could have ordered Jesus to do so. He
had to decide: Should he trust that Jesus could heal
simply by saying the words from afar? Yes, the nobleman decided. He believed Jesus had the miraculous
power to heal, and he trusted Jesus would do it. He
took Jesus at His word and headed home.

*Dear God, help me to believe You do amazing
miracles, even if I don't see You doing them
exactly the way I hoped. Amen.*

BRAVELY BELIEVING, PART 2

Jesus said to him, "Go your way. Your son will live."
The man put his trust in what Jesus said and left.
JOHN 4:50 NLV

♡♡

The nobleman headed back to his home in Capernaum, about twenty miles away. He was anxious and eager to get back to his son. While he was still traveling, some of his servants met him along the way. "Your son!" they cried. "He is alive!" The nobleman was filled with joy and relief! Then he asked, "What time did he get better?"

The servants said, "His fever left him yesterday at the seventh hour."

Wow! The father realized that was the *exact* time that Jesus had said to him, "Your son will live."

From then on, not only did the nobleman believe in Jesus, but so did everyone in his household. Because of the faith of a good father, many more were saved for believing in Jesus Christ.

Dear God, please remind me that when I bravely choose to believe in You, blessings come not just to me but to others around me when they see my faith. Amen.

STRONG SUIT

*Finally, let the mighty strength of the Lord make
you strong. Put on all the armor that God gives,
so you can defend yourself against the devil's tricks.
We are not fighting against humans. We are fighting
against forces and authorities and against rulers of
darkness and powers in the spiritual world. So put on
all the armor that God gives. Then when that evil day
comes, you will be able to defend yourself. And when
the battle is over, you will still be standing firm.*
EPHESIANS 6:10–13 CEV

♡♡

Do you have certain clothes you like to wear that when you put them on, you instantly feel more confident to face anything in your day? A favorite outfit that you know looks good and feels good too! An athlete ready to play feels more confident and brave with a uniform and gear too. And a soldier going to battle absolutely needs protective armor. God tells us that as Christians we need our strong suit on as well, a special kind of spiritual armor to wear as we fight the spiritual battles going on around us at all times.

*Dear God, thank You for wanting to protect and
equip us with exactly what we need to be strong,
brave, and able to fight against evil. Amen.*

READY TO GO

*Be ready! Let the truth be like a belt around your waist,
and let God's justice protect you like armor. Your desire
to tell the good news about peace should be like shoes
on your feet. Let your faith be like a shield, and you will
be able to stop all the flaming arrows of the evil one. Let
God's saving power be like a helmet, and for a sword
use God's message that comes from the Spirit.*
EPHESIANS 6:14–17 CEV

God's Word says to be dressed and ready to go in your
spiritual strong suit of armor. This scripture helps you
picture what it looks like and how it equips you to
stand firm in your faith and to share the good news of
Jesus with others—despite how our enemy the devil
wants to do everything he can to try to stop you. You
might even want to draw a picture of yourself in this
armor and tape it up where you get dressed every
morning. Then pray as you face your day like this:

*Dear God, I'm getting dressed for a new day
and putting Your special spiritual armor on top.
I'm prepared like You want me to be to stand strong
for You and share Your love with others. Amen.*

FIRST FLIGHT FEARS

All you who fear the LORD, trust the LORD!
He is your helper and your shield.
PSALM 115:11 NLT

♡ ♡

The very first time I ever flew on a plane, I was a teenager, and the flight was out of Cleveland, Ohio, headed to Denver, Colorado. The weather was not great—snowy and icy. I was nervous about my first flight anyway, and as we were seated on the plane, waiting to take off, suddenly greenish-colored goo started oozing down the windows on the outside of the plane. I sure wondered what on earth was going on and soon learned that the green goo was a liquid used to help keep ice off the plane. Well, that didn't make me feel any less nervous at all. It made me *extra* nervous! I kind of wanted to get off the plane and try again for my first flight in summertime when snow and ice shouldn't be a problem. But I did not run screaming from the plane. I trusted God and trusted that the pilots knew what they were doing and would do their best to fly us safely. They did, and the experience was a great lesson in remembering we are always in God's hands.

Dear God, please help me with my fears when I'm doing something new, and help me in weird situations too! Thank You! Amen.

TOTALLY TRANSFORMED, PART 1

*[Saul] fell to the ground. Then he heard a voice say,
"Saul, Saul, why are you working so hard against Me?"
Saul answered, "Who are You, Lord?" He said, "I am Jesus,
the One Whom you are working against. You hurt yourself
by trying to hurt Me." Saul was shaken and surprised.
Then he said, "What do You want me to do, Lord?"*
ACTS 9:4–6 NLV

♡♡

You've probably heard about the apostle Paul in the Bible, but do you know his story? He started out as someone known as Saul who was very religious, but he hated and killed believers in Christ Jesus. But then in a dramatic moment on the road to Damascus, Jesus stopped Paul in his tracks and changed him completely.

. . . .

*Dear God, I know You can work in dramatic ways in
people's lives. Help me always to be brave enough
to let You totally transform anything in me
that You see needs to change. Amen.*

TOTALLY TRANSFORMED, PART 2

The Lord said to [Saul], "Get up! Go into the city and you will be told what to do." Those with Saul were not able to say anything. They heard a voice but saw no one. Saul got up from the ground. When he opened his eyes, he saw nothing. They took him by the hand and led him to Damascus. He could not see for three days.

ACTS 9:6–9 NLV

♡♡

After God stopped Paul in his tracks, He caused Paul to go blind for a few days. With the help of a man named Ananias, God worked a total transformation in Paul and restored his sight. Soon Paul was a brand-new person and began spreading the good news that Jesus is the Son of God. He helped many people to know Him as Savior.

....

Dear God, when I see others who are so against You, remind me of Paul's story. I pray for people who work against You to have dramatic change in their lives and instead begin to love and serve You and preach You to others! I know nothing is impossible with You, God! Amen.

INSPIRED BY PAUL

*This letter is from Paul, a missionary of Jesus Christ.
God has sent me to tell that He has promised life
that lasts forever through Christ Jesus.*
2 TIMOTHY 1:1 NLV

Paul went on to do amazing things as he traveled and spread the good news of Jesus! And he wrote thirteen letters to encourage and teach Christians that are part of the books of God's Word in the New Testament today—Romans, 1 and 2 Corinthians, Galatians, Ephesians, Philippians, Colossians, 1 and 2 Thessalonians, 1 and 2 Timothy, Titus, and Philemon. Paul experienced many scary things, including shipwreck and prison time, on his journeys to teach people about Jesus, but he continued on in courage everywhere God led him. As you grow and study the Bible more, let Paul's life and his writings inspire you to be bold and brave too!

*Dear God, please help me to learn all I can
from the apostle Paul. Thank You for the
amazing work You did through him. Please
do amazing work through me too! Amen.*

IN THE HIGHEST HEAVENS, BUT HERE TO HELP

Our holy God lives forever in the highest heavens, and this is what he says: Though I live high above in the holy place, I am here to help those who are humble and depend only on me.
ISAIAH 57:15 CEV

♡♡

Imagine if you could pick up the phone and call the president of the United States and ask him for help with anything at any time. He's pretty powerful, right? So you would feel brave knowing that the president could come to your rescue for anything you asked. Even though not many of us are going to have close connection with important leaders, it doesn't matter—because we *do* have close connection and instant communication with the highest King of all time—our one true God who lives in the highest heavens! He promises He is here to help everyone who is humble and depends only on Him. Wow! That can make us feel brave for absolutely anything!

....

Dear God, You are the highest and best and most powerful of all, and yet You love me and want to help me. I am amazed and thankful, and I love You too! Amen.

INVISIBLE BUT NOT IMAGINARY

It was by faith that Moses left the land of Egypt,
not fearing the king's anger. He kept right on going
because he kept his eyes on the one who is invisible.
HEBREWS 11:27 NLT

♡♡

Maybe you had an imaginary friend when you were younger, an invisible pal with whom you could play games and be silly. As you grew older, you outgrew that "friend," but technically you actually do still have an invisible friend—though He is not imaginary or silly at all! The Bible talks about God being invisible, and this scripture specifically tells us that as Moses led God's people out of Egypt, he did not fear Pharaoh because he kept his eyes on our invisible God. The Bible also tells us to fix our eyes not on what we can see but on what we can't see (2 Corinthians 4:18). Real courage comes from real faith that God is who He says He is and loves and protects us, even when we can't always see Him with our human vision.

Dear God, You might be invisible to my eyes, but You
are not imaginary. I have seen and felt You working in
my life, protecting and loving me. Please keep showing
me more and grow my faith in You! Amen.

BRAVELY WORSHIPPING, PART 1

Around midnight Paul and Silas were praying
and singing hymns to God, and the
other prisoners were listening.
ACTS 16:25 NLT

On one of Paul's many travels, he and his friend Silas were put in jail. But this did not stop their faith in God. In fact, they used their jail time to pray and sing to God. Late at night while they were praying and singing and other prisoners were listening to them, suddenly an earthquake shook the jail. It was so strong that the prison doors flew open and everyone's chains broke loose!

Dear God, when I am in the middle of scary things, please
bring scripture and worship songs to my mind. I want to
sing and pray them back to You to keep my focus on You
and Your power to help in any kind of situation. Amen.

BRAVELY WORSHIPPING, PART 2

[The jailer's] entire household rejoiced because they all believed in God.
ACTS 16:34 NLT

♡♡

The jailer woke up and was terrified. He thought he would be killed for all the prisoners going free. But Paul said to him, "We are all here!" And the jailer ran to Paul and Silas and dropped to the ground in front of them. Then he brought them out of their jail cell and said, "What should I do to be saved?"

They told him, "Believe in the Lord Jesus, and you will be saved. You and your household."

And then the jailer took Paul and Silas to his home and fed them a meal. And everyone in his family listened to Paul and Silas and believed in Jesus.

....

Dear God, even in the worst circumstances, help me to be brave and keep worshipping You, just like Paul and Silas did. They saw a great miracle and helped others know You as Savior too! Amazing! Amen.

STRENGTH AND SO MUCH MORE

I love you, LORD; you are my strength. The LORD is
my rock, my fortress, and my savior; my God is my
rock, in whom I find protection. He is my shield,
the power that saves me, and my place of safety.
PSALM 18:1–2 NLT

Reading and focusing on scripture is one of the best
ways ever to fight fear and build courage! Even if you
just memorize verse 1 of Psalm 18, you have a simple
but powerful prayer to God for any kind of challenge
or trouble. And if you go on to memorize verse 2,
the passage will remind you that God is your

- strength,
- rock,
- fortress,
- Savior,
- shield,
- power, and
- place of safety.

When you set your mind on believing the bullet points
of that truth, there is no room for fear in your brain!

Dear God, keep bringing me back to Your Word to love and
learn. Fill up my brain with awesome power from scripture
so I can bravely kick out any worry or fear. Amen.

CREATOR OF ALL

"When you pass through the waters, I will be with you. When you pass through the rivers, they will not flow over you. When you walk through the fire, you will not be burned. The fire will not destroy you. For I am the Lord your God, the Holy One of Israel, Who saves you."
ISAIAH 43:2–3 NLV

♡♡

If you spend time learning about natural disasters, you could fill yourself with a lot of fear. Things like volcanic eruptions, tidal waves, earthquakes, hurricanes, tornadoes, and forest fires are fascinating— but frightening too. No human being can control or stop them from happening; we can only study them, watch out for them, and make emergency plans for safety during them. Natural disasters should be a reminder to people that no matter how great and smart we think we are, we can never control the earth or weather. So we should always be reaching out to the one true God who can control it all because He created it all. Even if natural disasters make us nervous, we can calm ourselves down in faith in our Creator God who loves and protects us with the promise of eternal life.

---

*Dear God, You are an awesome Creator,
and I trust in Your love and care! Amen.*

UNDER GOD'S PROTECTION

Live under the protection of God Most High and stay in the shadow of God All-Powerful. Then you will say to the LORD, "You are my fortress, my place of safety; you are my God, and I trust you." The Lord will keep you safe from secret traps and deadly diseases. He will spread his wings over you and keep you secure.
PSALM 91:1–4 CEV

Wow, these are powerful promises about how God takes care of us if we live under His protection. So how do we do that? First, we trust Him as the one true God. We believe in Jesus as our only Savior. We do our best to follow God's Word and live according to it. We stay in close relationship with our heavenly Father. All of that is awesome anyway, plus we receive many gifts of God's care on top!

Dear God, thank You for Your precious promises to me in Psalm 91! They give me so much courage! Amen.

BIG CHANGES AT SCHOOL

The LORD directs the steps of the godly. He delights in every detail of their lives. Though they stumble, they will never fall, for the LORD holds them by the hand.
PSALM 37:23–24 NLT

Have you ever had to change schools? My daughters, Jodi and Lilly, went from homeschooling to regular public school just this past year, and that took a lot of courage. We prayed for God to lead and direct, and saw Him answer in many cool ways. He also gave us wisdom to prepare as much as possible. We communicated well with school staff and set up tours and meetings beforehand to make the change go as smoothly as possible. God loves to help you through any kind of big change process too. Just ask Him, be patient to let Him work out His plans, and praise Him as you see Him work!

....

Dear God, if I ever have to change schools, please help me to be brave. Thank You! Amen.

CHANGE FOR A
NEW SCHOOL YEAR

For everything there is a season,
a time for every activity under heaven.
ECCLESIASTES 3:1 NLT

♡ ♡

Even if you're not changing actual schools, just the start of a brand-new school year can be scary. Will you be sad missing your old teacher? What will your new teacher be like? Who will be in your class, and will you find friends to get along well with? How much homework will there be? Have you experienced butterflies in your tummy thinking about any of this? I sure remember feeling nervous! But we can have courage when we remember that God oversees our days and our years. He is always guiding us through good days and bad and through each new school year.

· ·

Dear God, thank You for walking with me
and caring about all of my school days,
especially in a brand-new year! Amen.

CREEPING WORRIES, PART 1

I tell you not to worry about your life. Don't worry about having something to eat, drink, or wear. Isn't life more than food or clothing? Look at the birds in the sky! They don't plant or harvest. They don't even store grain in barns. Yet your Father in heaven takes care of them. Aren't you worth more than birds?
MATTHEW 6:25–26 CEV

Worries about all kinds of things can overtake your brain if you let them. So don't give worry to even the tiniest bit of your brain! Jesus' words about worry are very important. Read and focus on this scripture in Matthew 6 whenever you feel worries creeping near to take over your mind. Jesus' words will give you courage to defeat them.

Dear God, Your Word is so encouraging to remind me that You take care of all my needs and I don't need to worry about anything. Please bring this scripture to mind when I feel worries creeping near me. Amen.

CREEPING WORRIES, PART 2

Don't worry and ask yourselves, "Will we have anything to eat? Will we have anything to drink? Will we have any clothes to wear?" Only people who don't know God are always worrying about such things. Your Father in heaven knows that you need all of these. But more than anything else, put God's work first and do what he wants. Then the other things will be yours as well.
MATTHEW 6:31–33 CEV

♡♡

It's easy to try not to worry and then go right on worrying anyway. So what can you do? The scripture tells us to put God's work first! If you're focused on Him and what He wants you to do, then you won't have time for worries. Begin each day talking to God. Read the Bible and learn the good things He has for you. Do your best at school and on the tasks you are given from your parents and your teachers. Look for ways to love others like Jesus loves. When you focus on those things, there won't be room in your brain for worries to creep in!

Dear Jesus, help me to put You first in everything and leave no room for worries in my mind! Amen.

SNORKELING STORY, PART 1

Trust the LORD and live right! The land will be yours,
and you will be safe. Do what the LORD wants,
and he will give you your heart's desire.
PSALM 37:3–4 CEV

♡♡

One time on vacation I went on a sailboat seven miles off the coast of Key West, Florida, to snorkel over a coral reef. It was a wonderful experience! I'll admit, though, it was a little scary! No land was in sight, the water was deep, and all kinds of unpredictable ocean critters were swimming around. That's what we were there to see, after all! Our captain said there was a chance we could see sharks nearby too. So I went into the water planning not to venture too far from the boat and to stay near other people!

....

Dear God, help me to use wisdom and have good plans when I go into new situations that might hold some danger. I don't want to be too scared, but I also want to use caution! Thank You! Amen.

SNORKELING STORY, PART 2

Both of us need help. I can help make your faith strong and you can do the same for me. We need each other.
ROMANS 1:12 NLV

♡♡

I figured that if sharks came around, surely they wouldn't want to bother a big group of snorkelers, right? But I worried that if I went off by myself, I might be an easy target and end up as a shark snack! In the end we were totally safe during our hour or so of snorkel time, and I saw some beautiful ocean life! I had an amazing experience that made me stronger for facing some fears. But I've also thought how as Christians we need to keep other solid Christians near us in close friendship, just like I wanted to keep other snorkelers nearby for protection from any hungry sharks. Good friends who also follow Jesus can help surround us and keep us safe when we might be tempted to sin or go off by ourselves and be an easy target for the devil's attacks.

Dear God, please keep good Christian friends surrounding me. Help me to be wise to look for them and stay near them and not ever wander far away. Amen.

LOOK AT THE HEAVENS

*"To whom will you compare me? Who is my equal?"
asks the Holy One. Look up into the heavens. Who
created all the stars? He brings them out like an
army, one after another, calling each by its name.
Because of his great power and incomparable
strength, not a single one is missing.*
ISAIAH 40:25–26 NLT

♡♡

My daughter Jodi loves learning about outer space
and the planets and stars and black holes. She enjoys
using her telescope. And I love thinking about this
scripture when we look up at the night sky. When
we focus on how vast the sky is and how our God is
so much bigger that He actually has a name for each
star, it's mind-blowing! We can't help but be filled
with courage when we trust that the same great big
God who made the heavens and knows the stars by
name made us and knows our names and takes good
care of us too.

. . . .

*Dear God, I can't even wrap my mind around how
awesome You are! Thank You that I can talk to
You and depend on You for anything! Amen.*

THE SHIP WILL GO DOWN, PART 1

"But take courage! None of you will lose your lives, even though the ship will go down. For last night an angel of the God to whom I belong and whom I serve stood beside me, and he said, 'Don't be afraid, Paul. . . . God in his goodness has granted safety to everyone sailing with you.' So take courage! For I believe God. It will be just as he said. But we will be shipwrecked on an island."
ACTS 27:22–26 NLT

Paul was on a ship in a horrible storm, and his words to the crew and other passengers were comforting yet still a little scary. We might wonder, *Why didn't God just stop the storm completely? Why let them shipwreck at all?* We don't know for sure all the reasons why. But we can use this story as a reminder that God has never promised to always protect us from scary circumstances. Even in the midst of them, though, He can save our earthly lives. And what He does promise is heavenly life forever when we trust in Jesus as our one and only Savior.

Dear God, I don't always understand Your ways and why we go through scary things. But I want to keep trusting You anyway, and I know You ultimately save and give forever life to everyone who believes in Your Son. Amen.

THE SHIP WILL GO DOWN, PART 2

Once we were safe on shore, we learned that we were on the island of Malta. The people of the island were very kind to us. It was cold and rainy, so they built a fire on the shore to welcome us.
ACTS 28:1–2 NLT

Paul and everyone on board the ship were safe, just as the angel of God had promised. And we see how God provided for their needs through the good people of the island they landed on. No matter what hard or scary things you have to experience, God will always provide good people to help you through them too. Ask God to show you many blessings like this. Maybe it's the super nice nurse who helps you feel brave at the doctor's office. Or the assistant who helps you "get it" when you're totally stuck on division at school. Thank these people and praise God when you see Him working through others to take good care of you. It helps make you brave for any future hard thing too, because you have seen God take care of you in the past.

Dear God, thank You for always providing for my needs and bringing me helpers in every kind of situation. Amen.

MORNING, NOON, AND NIGHT

*I ask for your help, LORD God, and you will
keep me safe. Morning, noon, and night you
hear my concerns and my complaints.*
PSALM 55:16–17 CEV

It's good to have a set daily quiet time with God to
read the Bible and pray. But don't ever let that be the
only time you talk to God throughout the day. This
psalm reminds us that morning, noon, and night, God
hears any of our worries and fears. And He's ready to
listen at every moment in between as well as all night
long. If you wake up from a bad dream or a storm or
a strange noise, the very first thing you can do is cry
out to God in prayer for help and comfort! Isn't it
amazing that every single person in the world can
pray like this at any time too? What an awesome heavenly Father we have!

*Dear God, thank You for being available every
moment of every day to hear from me! Amen.*

WHEN WE DO WRONG

Come and listen, all you who fear God, and I will tell
you what he did for me. For I cried out to him for help,
praising him as I spoke. If I had not confessed the sin in
my heart, the Lord would not have listened. But God
did listen! He paid attention to my prayer.
PSALM 66:16–19 NLT

♡♡

To have total confidence that God listens and answers
our prayers, we must also regularly admit to God
when we do wrong things. That's called confessing
our sins. The Bible is clear that God forgives us and
removes our sin as far as the east is from the west
(Psalm 103:12), but we need to admit our sins to Him.
That keeps us humble and depending on God, which
is the best kind of confidence and courage, because
there is no one greater or more powerful than our
good and loving Father God!

Dear God, I do make many mistakes, and I don't
want to hide them or pretend like I don't. These
are my sins, God:_____. Please forgive me.
Thank You that You do! Amen.

DOGS VS. SQUIRRELS, PART 1

The Lord gives wisdom. Much learning and understanding come from His mouth. He stores up perfect wisdom for those who are right with Him.
PROVERBS 2:6–7 NLV

Our dogs, Jasper and Daisy, are obsessed with checking our backyard for renegade squirrels. Every time we let them out, they run as fast as they can to the corner of the yard where they most often find intruders. Just recently I saw a squirrel running for his life. Then suddenly he headed up a tree, then out on a limb, and jumped down on the ground right next to our fence and escaped to freedom before Jasper and Daisy even realized it. They were still barking up the tree, looking for him there. So funny!

I'm always kind of amazed that squirrels hang out in our yard when they know we have dogs as a threat. But the squirrels seem to have courage that comes from their ability to outsmart our pups.

Dear God, please give me the ability to outsmart my fears by using the best kind of wisdom that comes from You! Amen.

DOGS VS. SQUIRRELS, PART 2

Happy is the person who finds wisdom. And happy is the person who gets understanding. Wisdom is worth more than silver. It brings more profit than gold. Wisdom is more precious than rubies. Nothing you want is equal to it. With her right hand wisdom offers you a long life. With her left hand she gives you riches and honor. Wisdom will make your life pleasant. It will bring you peace. As a tree makes fruit, wisdom gives life to those who use it. Everyone who uses wisdom will be happy.

PROVERBS 3:13–18 ICB

Now when I watch dogs versus squirrel battles in my backyard, I think of it as a fun reminder that keeping our brains healthy and sharp is a great way to have more courage. And the best way to keep our brains healthy and sharp is to keep asking our loving Creator for more and more of His wisdom. This passage in Proverbs talks about the many benefits of finding wisdom!

Dear God, please grow my mind in faith and in Your love and wisdom and help me outsmart any worry or fear. Amen.

CONFIDENT AND FEARLESS

*[Those who fear the Lord] do not fear bad
news; they confidently trust the Lord to care
for them. They are confident and fearless.*
Psalm 112:7–8 NLT

♡♡

Can this be said of you? I'm not sure it always can be said of me, but I want it to be! The words in this psalm are something every Christian should want to be said of them. If you go back to the beginning at Psalm 112:1, it will tell you that it's the people who fear the Lord and are happy to obey His commands that this is true of. Then we have the promise of God's care. He doesn't want bad attitudes; He wants us to enjoy obeying Him because His commands are the wisest and best way to live a good life here on earth and then a perfect life in heaven. Loving and obeying God makes us confident and fearless now and forever!

*Dear God, thank You for Your commands.
I always want to be happy to obey them! Amen.*

PERFECT PEACE

You will keep in perfect peace all who trust in you,
all whose thoughts are fixed on you! Trust in the Lord
always, for the Lord God is the eternal Rock.
Isaiah 26:3–4 NLT

Perfect peace almost sounds way too good to be true in this world. There always seems to be something ruining our peace, even if it's just a sibling squabble or an annoying classmate or a huge homework assignment. But God's Word tells us how to have perfect peace—by trusting in God and fixing our thoughts on Him. When we feel our peace being disrupted, we need to turn our attention back to God and ask for His help to handle what's causing the stress. Perfect peace is pretty priceless (and a tongue-twister!).

. . . .

Dear God, I trust You and would love to have
perfect peace all the time. Please help me to
turn my thoughts back to You in stressful
situations and keep them there! Amen.

LIGHT OF THE WORLD

"You are the light of the world—like a city on a hilltop that cannot be hidden. No one lights a lamp and then puts it under a basket. Instead, a lamp is placed on a stand, where it gives light to everyone in the house. In the same way, let your good deeds shine out for all to see, so that everyone will praise your heavenly Father."
MATTHEW 5:14–16 NLT

What a beautiful thing to get up and tell yourself each morning as you look in the mirror, "You are the light of the world." That's what Jesus has said of you and me when we trust Him as Savior. With the Holy Spirit in us, our job is to shine our lights so that others will want to trust Jesus as Savior and praise God too! We don't ever want to cover up our light. The dark world around us needs the good news and love of Jesus so very much, so let's do good things and be brave to shine as brightly as we can!

Dear Jesus, thank You for calling me the light of the world. I want to shine Your love brightly to everyone around me and give God all the praise! Amen.

BRAVE FOR BIG CHANGES, PART 1

Jesus Christ is the same yesterday,
today, and forever.
HEBREWS 13:8 NLT

Our family moved a couple of years ago, and we learned that moving brings huge changes. New house, new neighborhood, new church, new people, new schools. Maybe you feel excited and adventurous about change, or maybe change makes you feel anxious and scared. Either way is okay because it's good to be you and listen to what you're feeling! Then you can take those feelings to God and pray about them. Ask Him to help you deal wisely with change and have the courage to learn and grow and adjust the way He wants you to. And ask Him to show you all the good new plans He has for you in your time of change.

Dear God, please help me when my life is changing in big ways. Thank You that You always stay the same and I can depend on You no matter what. Amen.

BRAVE FOR BIG CHANGES, PART 2

"I am the LORD, and I do not change."
MALACHI 3:6 NLT

Even if your life does not have major changes, life is full of small changes year to year and even day to day. Think about how you get new teachers and leaders at school and church as you get older. Think about how you grow out of toys and activities you used to love when you were younger. Change can feel overwhelming at times, so it's wonderful to remember that God promises He never changes. He is our one solid constant no matter what new things are going on in our lives. Maybe even though you outgrow toys, you have that one special stuffed animal that you never get tired of and is *always* comforting to hug. You could sort of think of God like that one unchanging stuffed animal that always brings you comfort through the ups and downs of life. And even better, God is *far, far* more awesome and loving to you!

Dear God, thank You for being a constant comfort and help to me! You are always my source of courage! Amen.

WALK WITH THE WISE

Walk with the wise and become wise;
associate with fools and get in trouble.
PROVERBS 13:20 NLT

Think about the bravest people you know. What makes you think they are brave? Is it their job? Is it the hard things they have gone through? Is it how they take care of others? While you're young it's a great idea to get in the habit now of asking smart and respectful questions to grown-ups you think are brave. Ask them how they got into the job they are in. Or ask what it was like to endure the hard thing they went through. Be willing and happy to have good and deep conversations with grown-ups so that you can learn lessons from those who are older and wiser than you.

Dear God, please show me the brave and wise people in my life from whom I need to learn. Thank You for their courage, and help me to build more courage too. Amen.

BRAVE TO BREAK IT OFF

Don't make friends with anyone who has a bad temper.
You might turn out like them and get caught in a trap.
PROVERBS 22:24–25 CEV

♡♡

Sometimes, sadly, you have to be brave to break off bad friendships. If a friend you're close to starts making lots of wrong choices or treating others badly, it's not good to stay close friends. You don't want them to drag you down and into sin or trouble. God's Word certainly tells us to share love and kindness and love our enemies, but it also says, "Bad friends will destroy you" (1 Corinthians 15:33 CEV). We need wisdom to know how to show love to others without also joining others in sin. And sometimes the bravest thing to do is to peacefully say to someone, "We just can't be friends anymore."

. . . .

Dear God, please give me wisdom about
friendships, and help me to have the courage
to end a friendship if I need to. Amen.

RIDING THE RAPIDS

Have faith in God, who is rich and blesses us
with everything we need to enjoy life.
1 TIMOTHY 6:17 CEV

Just once I went white-water rafting, and it was a great time. I was with a friend in beautiful Montana, and the company and scenery were spectacular! The rafting was a little scary, though, even though we had picked an easy course and had a wonderful guide. It's just a little nerve-wracking to know you might fall out of a raft into churning rapids, freezing water, and lots of rocks! But thankfully none of our group ever fell out of the raft, and I'm glad for the experience. Braving new things is good for building your character and helping you be strong and confident. That doesn't mean you have to do crazy daredevil things, of course. Just ask God to give you wisdom and show you the cool experiences that would be good for you to have throughout your life!

....

Dear God, thank You for making the world so full of cool
things to do! Guide me and make me brave for trying new
things and learning and growing through them. Amen.

TO THE RESCUE, PART 1

I come to you, LORD, for protection. Don't let me be ashamed. Do as you have promised and rescue me. Listen to my prayer and hurry to save me. Be my mighty rock and the fortress where I am safe.
PSALM 31:1–2 CEV

♡♡

My daughter Lilly had a moment on her sixth birthday that terrified her. We were driving home from the store, and she suddenly saw a stink bug crawling up her seat belt toward her face. Stink bugs aren't dangerous to people, but when you're six years old and you can't get away from one because you're stuck in your seat belt in a moving car, they can seem deadly! This one did to Lilly. I was driving and couldn't help her, so that made her all the more scared. When the stink bug kept creeping closer to her face, she started crying so hard that I found a place to pull over and came to the rescue.

. . . .

Dear God, thank You for providing people to come to my rescue. It gives me courage to know You see everything and You help at exactly the right time. Amen.

TO THE RESCUE, PART 2

The Lord hears his people when they call to him for help.
He rescues them from all their troubles.
PSALM 34:17 NLT

♡♡

Right after I stopped to come to Lilly's rescue, a police officer also pulled over to make sure we were okay—all because of a silly little stink bug! I laugh at that story now, but Lilly doesn't really think it's funny. She still remembers the fear, and she still *really* hates stink bugs. What's even better to remember, though, is how she ended up just fine and to think of the experience as a lesson that God always provides rescue and sometimes even extra help on top!

Thank You for being our best rescuer,
Father! In any scary situation, I know You
are watching and will provide, sometimes
even above and beyond what I need. Amen.

SIMPLE BUT POWERFUL

Be on guard. Stand firm in the faith. Be courageous.
Be strong. And do everything with love.
1 CORINTHIANS 16:13–14 NLT

These words from Paul to the Christians in Corinth are good for us to remember today. We should be on guard against the devil's attacks and temptation to sin. We should stand firm and not let anyone pull us away from our faith. We should be courageous and strong, knowing that God never leaves us and is always helping us. And we should do everything in love so that others might want to know the love of Christ Jesus too.

....

Dear God, help me to memorize these simple but
powerful words. I want to be on guard, stand firm,
be courageous and strong, and do everything in love.
That seems like a wonderful "code" to live by! Amen.

MAKE WORK FUN

Work willingly at whatever you do, as though you were working for the Lord rather than for people.
COLOSSIANS 3:23 NLT

What's your attitude about helping with new chores around the house? Are you eager to learn, or are you whiny and lazy about it? What if from now on you think about it as a brave thing to do? It does take some courage to learn any new thing, even if it's just a household task. So if Mom says, "I'm going to teach you to clean out the refrigerator well," or if Dad says, "I'm going to teach you to mow the lawn" you have a choice to complain or to think of it as a brave new adventure. Absolutely, it might take some extreme imagination, but your attitude toward work makes a huge difference in your life. If you can make it fun and find ways to enjoy it, you are one smart cookie!

Dear God, help me to think of learning any new thing as a brave new adventure. Thank You for giving me a brain that's so capable of learning! Amen.

WONDERFULLY MADE

*You created my inmost being; you knit me together
in my mother's womb. I praise you because I am
fearfully and wonderfully made; your works
are wonderful, I know that full well.*
PSALM 139:13–14 NIV

This is a popular scripture and a great one to remember! God made you and has known every detail about you since the moment you first began life in your mother's tummy. That should give you great courage and confidence that you are well-known and loved by the Creator of the universe. Call out to God in praise for the awesome way He has made you. Talk to Him constantly about the wonderful works He has done and the ones He wants to continue to do through you.

*Dear God, I'm amazed at how You know and love me!
I don't think I can fully understand it, but I never
want to stop trying to know You better. Amen.*

A HUG GONE WRONG

The Lord is near to those who have a broken heart.
PSALM 34:18 NLV

One of my earliest memories was in a crowded bathroom at church when I was just three or four years old. There were so many ladies all around me, and I felt overwhelmed and shy. I hugged the pair of legs closest to me and then looked up to see a stranger's face! This was not my mom! And these were not her legs! I let go and began to cry. When everyone else laughed, I just felt worse—embarrassed on top of scared.

My mom quickly found me, and all was soon fine, but I will never forget that scary feeling that she was gone and a stranger had taken her place. My mom is in heaven now, and I miss her terribly. But I'm so thankful that I will spend forever with her in heaven because she knew Jesus as her Savior. And I have confidence and courage because of the way God has shown me His love in extra-special ways because He knows I miss my mom. He will show you His love in extra-special ways when you go through difficult times too.

....

Dear God, hug me close to You when I experience scary and embarrassing and hard and sad things in my life. Thank You! Amen.

NOT BACKWARD AT ALL

*Jesus taught the people and said, ". . .Those who are
sad now are happy. God will comfort them. Those who
are humble are happy. The earth will belong to them.
Those who want to do right more than anything else
are happy. God will fully satisfy them. . . . Those who
are treated badly for doing good are happy. The
kingdom of heaven belongs to them."*
MATTHEW 5:2–10 ICB

Have you ever played "opposite day" or maybe had
"backward day" at school? Sometimes I think of the
Beatitudes in Jesus' Sermon on the Mount as seem-
ing like they are opposite or backward teaching com-
pared to the teaching of the world. But thankfully
His teaching is not actually backward at all. It shows
how good God is to take the hard things of this life
and present them as positives to us—because He will
make everything good and right in the end when we
have perfect life with Him forever in heaven. That
gives us great courage to face anything in life.

*Dear God, thank You for Your teaching in the Sermon on
the Mount. Help me to keep learning and experiencing
more and more how this teaching is true! Amen.*

SERVING JESUS

"When did we give you something to eat or drink? When did we welcome you as a stranger or give you clothes to wear or visit you while you were sick or in jail?" The king will answer, "Whenever you did it for any of my people, no matter how unimportant they seemed, you did it for me."
MATTHEW 25:37–40 CEV

Our family recently served together with other families from our church at a shelter for homeless people. We did a simple project of coloring encouraging scripture cards to go with the free meals provided to those in need. God's Word tells us that even the smallest thing done for others is as if we're serving Jesus Himself. So never be afraid to step up and serve others in need. As you try new things that might feel a little scary, remember that you are actually serving Jesus. You know He loves you, and there's nothing to be afraid of when drawing closer to Him.

Dear God, please show me the opportunities You want me to take to help others. Help me never to be afraid as I serve in Your name to share Your great love. Amen.

SPEAK UP BOLDLY

Some argued, "He's a good man," but others said,
"He's nothing but a fraud who deceives the people."
But no one had the courage to speak favorably
about him in public, for they were afraid of
getting in trouble with the Jewish leaders.
JOHN 7:12–13 NLT

When Jesus was teaching on earth, some people who heard Him were interested and thought He was a good man, but they let fear keep them quiet. They didn't want to get in trouble with the Jewish leaders who were saying Jesus was a liar and a fake. As you grow and mature, ask God to help you never to be afraid of anyone who says Jesus is a fake. Those people might seem powerful in this world to tease you and hurt you, but they are never more powerful than God. They are never more powerful than the good plans He has for you when you stay close to Him and stand strong in your faith. Speak up for Jesus and bravely tell others about Him, how He has saved you, and all the good things He is doing in your life.

Dear Jesus, I am proud of You, and I never want to
be scared of anyone who says I shouldn't be proud
of You! You are my Savior, and I love You! Amen.

FULL OF COURAGE FOR
CHRIST'S RETURN

*The Spirit teaches you everything you need to know,
and what he teaches is true—it is not a lie. So just as
he has taught you, remain in fellowship with Christ.
And now, dear children, remain in fellowship with
Christ so that when he returns, you will be full of
courage and not shrink back from him in shame.*
1 JOHN 2:27–28 NLT

♡♡

As Christians we are supposed to be ready for Jesus
to return to earth at any time (Matthew 24:44; Luke
12:40). For some that might sound scary, but for
those of us who stay close to Jesus, it should be exciting! It should fill us with joy and hope! This scripture
talks about how if we remain in fellowship with Jesus,
meaning in close connection, then we will be full of
courage and not shrink back with fear or be ashamed
in any way when Jesus returns to earth.

*Dear Jesus, please keep me close to You. Help me to
make good habits of spending time with You and to
want more and more good fellowship with You! Amen.*

PROVEN FAITH

*God gave us the courage to declare his Good News
to you boldly, in spite of great opposition. So you can
see we were not preaching with any deceit or impure
motives or trickery. For we speak as messengers
approved by God to be entrusted with the Good
News. Our purpose is to please God, not people.
He alone examines the motives of our hearts.*
1 THESSALONIANS 2:2–4 NLT

When we suffer through hard things and still trust
God and share the good news of Jesus, we help prove
to others the truth that Jesus really is the one and
only Savior and Son of God. We show others that He
is worth believing in. God gives us the courage to
share the Gospel boldly, no matter our situation. Just
ask Him and trust Him! He knows your heart and your
goal should always be to please Him and not other
people.

*Dear God, I want to help others see the absolute
truth of Your good news that Jesus is our one and
only Savior. If I have to go through hard and scary
times to help prove that, then I will, so please
fill me up with great courage. Amen.*

A COWARDLY MISTAKE

A servant girl noticed him in the firelight and
began staring at him. Finally she said, "This man
was one of Jesus' followers!" But Peter denied it.
"Woman," he said, "I don't even know him!"
LUKE 22:56–57 NLT

We can learn lessons from people who acted cowardly—about what *not* to do. The same Peter who was the brave one to step out and walk toward Jesus on water was also the one who later denied even knowing Jesus. Three times, actually! When Jesus had been arrested and was about to be crucified, Peter felt too afraid of what the people might do to him if he showed loyalty to Jesus. And then Peter felt awful for denying his Lord whom he actually loved so much. The Bible says he cried bitterly. Jesus still loved Peter after this mistake, but we need to do our very best not to make the same mistake. Jesus is loyal to us, and we should always be loyal to Him—and never ashamed of calling Him our Lord and Savior.

Dear Jesus, please keep me so close to You that I
could never deny knowing and loving You! Amen.

THE GREATEST ACT OF COURAGE, PART 1

Jesus walked on a little way before he knelt down and prayed, "Father, if you will, please don't make me suffer by having me drink from this cup. But do what you want, and not what I want." Then an angel from heaven came to help him. Jesus was in great pain and prayed so sincerely that his sweat fell to the ground like drops of blood.
LUKE 22:41–44 CEV

There is no greater act of courage than when Jesus gave up His life for us. It sure wasn't easy for Him. A hard but good passage of scripture to read is where Jesus was crying out to God in the Garden of Gethsemane just before He was arrested and then crucified. In His time of prayer in the garden, He asked His Father God if there might be another way so that He didn't have to suffer. But He also said to God, "Do what you want, and not what I want."

Dear Jesus, please help me always to be brave enough to pray like You did to God, saying "Do what You want, not what I want." Amen.

THE GREATEST ACT
OF COURAGE, PART 2

Around noon the sky turned dark and stayed that way
until the middle of the afternoon. The sun stopped shining,
and the curtain in the temple split down the middle. Jesus
shouted, "Father, I put myself in your hands!" Then he died.
LUKE 23:44–46 CEV

Jesus was willing to do anything Father God wanted
because He knew God's ways are always best and always working out good for people who love Him. And
in this case, God was working through Jesus' suffering to save all people from their sins. The most courageous act of all time was also the saddest act of all
time—for Jesus was guilty of nothing yet took on all
our sin—but it was also the most loving act of all time.

Dear Jesus, help me never to forget Your greatest act
of courage to save all people from their sin. Help me
to share bravely what You did to give us eternal life so
that more and more people will trust in You! Amen.

THE GREATEST ACT OF COURAGE, PART 3

Two men in shining white clothes. . .said, "Why are you looking in the place of the dead for someone who is alive? Jesus isn't here! He has been raised from death."
LUKE 24:4–6 CEV

The greatest act of courage of all time ended with the greatest victory of all time—when Jesus conquered death forever by coming back to life. Only the one true God could ever accomplish this! And because we have the hope of this exact kind of win over death, we can live without fear of anything! God is almighty Creator and our loving heavenly Father; He sent His Son Jesus to teach us how to live our lives and to be the payment for our sins; and He gave us the Holy Spirit to be with us and guide us constantly until we spend forever in heaven. We have everything we need because of Jesus' greatest act of courage, and we can do our best to live each of our days courageously too.

Dear God, I have everything I need in You and Your Son and Your Holy Spirit. I am full of power and courage because of Your great love and gift of eternal life! Thank You, thank You, thank You! Amen.

COURAGE TO SHARE
THE GOOD NEWS

*For I am not ashamed of this Good News
about Christ. It is the power of God at work,
saving everyone who believes.*
ROMANS 1:16 NLT

Anyone who knows the saving love of Jesus should never be ashamed or scared to share Him with others. We know the very best news the world has ever heard, and we need to be bold to share it. The best news ever is that God sent His perfect Son, Jesus, to earth to live among us and show His love and then die for us as payment for our sin. Then He rose again to show how God gives eternal life to all who believe in Him! Ask God to make you bold and brave to share that awesome good news with as many others as you can!

....

*Dear God, I never want to be ashamed of the good
news of Jesus and how we can have eternal life
because You love us so much. Make me bold and
brave to share Your truth and love! Amen.*

SCRIPTURE INDEX

OLD TESTAMENT

MORE BOOKS FOR COURAGEOUS GIRLS!

Dare to Be a Courageous Girl

This delightfully unique journal will challenge you to live boldly for God! With each turn of the page, you will encounter a new "dare" from the easy-to-understand New Life Version of scripture alongside a brief devotional reading and thought-provoking journal prompt or "challenge" that encourages you to take action and obey God's Word.

Paperback / 978-1-64352-642-3 / $14.99

The Bible for Courageous Girls

Part of the exciting Courageous Girls series, this Bible provides complete Old and New Testament text in the easy-reading New Life™ Version, plus insert pages featuring full-color illustrations of bold, brave women such as Abigail, Deborah, Esther, Mary Magdalene, and Mary, mother of Jesus.

DiCarta / 978-1-64352-069-8 / $24.99

With your parent's permission, check out
CourageousGirls.com where you'll discover additional positive, faith-building activities and resources!